Contemporary
Cayce

Contemporary Cayce

A Complete Exploration Using Today's Philosophy and Science

Kevin J. Todeschi
and
Henry Reed

A.R.E. Press

A.R.E. Press • Virginia Beach • Virginia

Contents

" . . . there is being laid out plans for a work that, as given, is to change the thought of mankind in general in many directions." (254-37)   Edgar Cayce

1

An Overview of the Edgar Cayce Material

EDGAR CAYCE (1877–1945) HAS BEEN CALLED "THE SLEEPING prophet," "the father of holistic medicine," "the miracle man of Virginia Beach," and "the most-documented psychic of all time." For forty-three years of his adult life, he had the ability to put himself into some kind of self-induced sleep state by lying down on a couch, closing his eyes, and folding his hands over his stomach. This state of relaxation and meditation enabled him to place his mind in contact with all time and space and gave him the ability to respond to any question he was asked. His responses came to be called "readings" and contained insights so valuable that even to this day Edgar Cayce's work is known throughout the world. Hundreds of books have explored his amazing psychic gift, and the entire range of Cayce material is accessed by tens of thousands of people each and every day.

For decades, the Cayce readings have stood the test of time, research, and extensive study. Further details of Cayce's life and work are explored in such classic books as *There Is a River* (1942) by Thomas Sugrue, *The Sleeping Prophet* (1967) by Jess Stearn, *Many Mansions* (1950) by Gina Cerminara, *Edgar Cayce: A Seer Out of Season* (1990) by Harmon Bro, and *Ed-*

1

gar Cayce: An American Prophet (2000) by Sidney Kirkpatrick. (Further information about Edgar Cayce is available from the nonprofit he founded in 1931, the Association for Research and Enlightenment [A.R.E.]. Visit the Edgar Cayce's A.R.E. web site at EdgarCayce.org.)

During Cayce's life, the Edgar Cayce readings were all numbered to provide confidentiality. So in the case of 294-1, for example, the first set of numbers ("294") refers to the individual or group for whom the reading was given. The second set of numbers ("1") refers to the number in the series from which the reading is taken. Therefore, 294-1 identifies the reading as the first one given to the individual assigned #294.

Although the vast majority of the Cayce material deals with health and every manner of illness, countless topics were explored by Cayce's psychic talent: dreams, philosophy, intuition, business advice, the Bible, education, childrearing, ancient civilizations, reincarnation, personal spirituality, improving human relationships, finding your mission in life, and much more. In fact, during Cayce's lifetime, his readings covered an amazing 10,000 different subjects! However, this broad range of subject matter can be categorized into a smaller range of topical areas, such as the following:

- We have the capacity to improve our own **health**.
- Our individual relationships (home, work, everywhere) are our ongoing research laboratory in **personal soul growth**.
- We have an innate ability to obtain **personal guidance** at any time (dreams, intuition, synchronicities, etc.)
- Whatever life experience we are encountering right now is ultimately purposeful with the goal being one of **consciousness growth** for having had that experience.
- Through attunement (especially **meditation and prayer**), we can come to an understanding of our personal relationship with God.
- Experiences of various **changes in our life** are often at the core of promoting changes in our consciousness and personal growth.
- We do not come into life as blank slate—we are an archaeological dig of **ancient mysteries**.
- **We are loved** (and assisted) by the Creator.
- **We are eternal**.

In terms of health, the Cayce information was decades ahead of its time in exploring topics such as energy medicine, the importance of a healthy diet, the role of attitudes and emotions in the wellness process, and the important role various schools of medicine played in promoting health. Although Cayce himself has been called the "father of holistic medicine," the readings draw from every school of medicine: allopathic, osteopathic, chiropractic, physical therapy; and every imaginable treatment: surgery, diet, massage, exercise, pharmacological, mindfulness, vibrational therapies, meditation and prayer, and much more. In fact, the creation of the short-lived Cayce hospital (1928–1931) was the fulfillment of Edgar Cayce's dream in which all schools of medicine could work together for the benefit of the patient.

In 1931, a group of Cayce's contemporaries began obtaining a series of readings on the topic of personal soul growth. The first lesson was on "Cooperation," followed by "Know Thyself," "Spiritual Ideals," and so forth, and for more than a decade the group would explore a series of twenty-four ecumenical lessons in personal transformation. It was the group's hope that, regardless of an individual's religious background, universal concepts might somehow be practically applied as a means of becoming consciously aware of the living Spirit in everyday life. Today that information continues to be explored and applied by A.R.E. Study Groups and individuals around the world.

A wealth of information in the Cayce files examines the innate capacity that each of us has to obtain personal guidance into any area of our lives. This aptitude for guidance occurs because the mind and consciousness are not limited to the confines of the physical world or the body. Actually, Cayce suggested that, in terms of dreams, nothing of significance ever occurs to us without it first being foreshadowed in our dreams. He also asserted that everyone had the ability to interpret, or make constructive use of their dreams. The readings also contend that ultimately each individual is actually his or her own best psychic, with an abundance of potential information and insight that is just waiting to come to conscious awareness. Because the universe wants us to succeed in our personal growth and development, we are also constantly greeted with "signs along way"—experiences, encounters, surprise happenings, etc., that can serve as synchronistic guidance that appears just when we need it.

Although it can be challenging to comprehend (and obviously much harder to experience), the Cayce material suggests that each of us is where we are right now for a reason. At some level, all of life's challenges have been chosen by the soul for the purpose of consciousness growth and development. Rather than seeing this dynamic as some kind of "punishment," the readings instead contend that this process ultimately enables individuals to become more compassionate, more loving, and more capable of helping others with the very same issue.

Edgar Cayce saw meditation as quieting the self and listening to the Spirit within. Prayer is a counterpart to meditation that enables an individual to communicate with the divine—ultimately not *asking for* things but instead *asking to* be used as a channel of blessings to someone else. The physical body and the mind can be used as a channel for vibrational healing energy. In fact, Cayce stated that healing energy could be disseminated on "the wings of thought." For years, the readings explored meditation, prayer, and personal affirmations as tools for attunement that could elicit a "closer walk" with God. That information makes it very clear that the divine can and does speak to all individuals regardless of religious background.

Throughout the years that he gave readings, people just like you and me approached Cayce and asked about all kinds of changes: changes in employment (losing one's job), changes in relationships (divorce or the loss of a loved one), changes in personal finances or in the economy, even global changes (such as earthquakes or enormous weather changes). And although the readings gave guidance that was very personal to each of these individuals, the underlying philosophy seemed to be one in which whatever changes an individual was experiencing in life were often tied to the opportunity for personal change and growth. In other words, external events often take place as a means of facilitating internal change and consciousness growth.

After health, the second most popular topic covered by the readings was the subject of reincarnation. The emphasis from the readings' perspective is not on who an individual was in the past but instead upon the fact that all of our abilities and frailties, as well as our experiences and relationships, remained within our soul's memory as a pool of information and knowledge that each of us can draw upon and learn from in the present. When individuals received "Life" readings, which dealt with the soul's entire life through various incarnations, the readings would essentially trace their soul histories from the earliest periods of Creation or Atlantis, and then follow their individual journeys and the lessons they had learned as well as those they still needed to obtain through approximately five or six major periods in history, focusing only upon those lifetimes that were the most important to the individual at that time in the present. It was this approach that led to massive amounts of data on ancient civilizations, prehistory, and information that suggests there has been an ever-evolving growth in human consciousness.

The readings are unequivocal in their stance that the Creator is both a very loving parent as well as an all-encompassing Force. With this in mind, we are loved and assisted by the Creator, who is desirous of us coming to a full understanding of our rightful place as "godlings"— children of the divine with an inherent capacity for compassion and co-creation. Cayce was just as adamant in the premise that since we are all Children of the same Creator, the divine loves us all equally.

Finally, the readings contend that, as spiritual beings, we are eternal. That spiritual part of us is everlasting, perpetual, and timeless, just as our Creator.

Ultimately, the overreaching philosophy of all of the Edgar Cayce material is the Oneness of God, the spiritual nature of humankind, and the purposefulness of all life. Taken together, these three components stand at the heart of the Cayce information and might best be described as the Cayce Cosmology.

In terms of Oneness, the readings suggest that every spiritual path should begin with a six-month lesson on Oneness: the Oneness of God, the Oneness of all Force, the ultimate Oneness of our connection to and responsibility for one another, and so forth. Although Cayce himself was a Christian, he very clearly understood that religion was essentially associated with the *form* whereas one's personal spirituality was best associated with the *application*. On one occasion when the readings were asked to respond to a question regarding religious orthodoxy, the response came: "What is the difference? As He has given, it will ever be found that Truth . . . is of the One Source. Are there not trees of oak, of ash, of pine? There are the needs of these for meeting this or that experience . . . all will fill their place. Find not fault with any but rather show forth as to how good a pine, or ash, or oak, or vine, thou art!" (254-87)

The spiritual nature of humankind is perhaps best summarized with the statement that we are not physical beings who happen to have a soul, but we are instead spiritual beings currently inhabiting a physical body. The purpose behind this physical consciousness experience is ultimately to bring the divine into the earth. From Cayce's premise, we are essentially divine emissaries charged with bringing spirit into the third dimension. Obviously, the chaos in much of the world suggests that we are collectively not living up to our destiny but nonetheless that is who we are and what we are supposed to be about. The readings suggest that the best example of living a full embodiment of the spirit while in the earth was demonstrated by Jesus. Cayce called Jesus our elder brother, a soul who fully demonstrated the living awareness of the spirit in the earth—something each of us is called to do. Therefore, regardless of one's religious form, the example of Jesus' life can be helpful to everyone. The readings called this example a "pattern" and stated: "For all have the pattern, whether they call on that name or not."

Life is a purposeful experience both individually and collectively. As already stated, individually it is purposeful in that all of our life events are designed with our own growth and development in mind. Another way of approaching this concept is to understand that an individual's life is not created by the things that happen to her or him but instead an individual's life is created by the way he or she responds to the things that happen during life's unfoldment. Collectively, we are charged with transforming the planet in whatever sphere we find ourselves.

Throughout his life, Edgar Cayce claimed no special abilities, nor did he ever consider himself to be some kind of twentieth-century prophet. The readings never offered a set of beliefs that had to be embraced, but instead focused on the fact that each person should test in his or her own life the principles presented. Though Cayce himself was a Christian and read the Bible from cover to cover every year of his life, his work was one that stressed the importance of comparative study among belief systems all over the world. The underlying principle of the readings is the oneness of all life, a tolerance for all people, and a compassion and understanding for every major religion in the world.

2

Oneness: An Idea that Will Change the World

WHEN PEOPLE CONSULTED EDGAR CAYCE CONCERNING THEIR problems, his response was often to turn things on their head, giving an unexpected way to look at the situation. People would come to him with their likes and dislikes, their hopes and fears, what they wanted and what they didn't want, and his answer would often put things into a different perspective, shifting the focus from the outer circumstance and its challenge to attitude and growth. One of the most important of these "revisionist" ideas was his concept of "Oneness." Although there are many levels to his premise, what he means by this idea is likely to have tremendous implications in terms of how individuals perceive, respond to, and experience the world. Ultimately, it is an ancient idea whose time has finally come in a way that can truly change the thought of humankind.

Cayce often quoted the phrase from the Bible, "The Lord thy God is One!" (Deuteronomy 6:4, KJV) We might think of this statement as claiming that there is a God, but only one God. True enough; and Cayce affirmed this aspect of Oneness many times. There is only One force in the universe, he insisted. He meant it, and to prove it he repeatedly noted that even what we think of as "evil" is nevertheless part of that same one force, just misapplied. Yet he also meant something much more radical than the one-God idea. For Cayce, Oneness also meant that everything, all that is, and all that ever will be, is One—one force, one substance, one being, one reality—and that reality is God. There is nothing in existence that is not God. This idea is revolutionary, and it might take some working up to in order to be able to grasp it clearly and fully.

Let's start with something suggested by Edgar Cayce. He recommended that the start of every spiritual or religious search begin with a six-month lesson on oneness. This might take on numerous approaches. Let's look, for example, at the oneness of humanity. On the one hand, we can meditate on our common qualities. As in the Buddhist compassion meditation, we can remember that "others have hopes for their lives, just as I do" or "others feel pain, just as I do" and so on. At a more profound level, we may realize that although our skin provides us with a biological boundary, we are constantly exchanging molecules with our environment. Not only are the green plants giving off oxygen molecules, which we then incorporate into our bodies, the wind blows our exhaled molecules around the world. Scientists have speculated that almost everyone on the planet has molecules within them from many, many other people in the world. Humanity shares the same ingredients for making their bodies.

Generally speaking, science knows that the planet itself and all life on the planet are engaged in a molecule exchange program. Although our eyes learn to see boundaries, such as the bark that surrounds a tree, the feathers that surround a bird, and the skin that surrounds us, all living beings are extracting needed substances from the environment (such as humans needing to breathe oxygen) and giving off unneeded substances that are in turn needed by other life forms (such as all of us exhaling carbon dioxide, which is used by plants). The planet is one living being, and we are a part of this whole. Cayce constantly reminds us to be mindful of what we are putting out and what we are taking in. People in the "green" movement express the same sentiment today, being concerned about everything from what is in our food to what we put into the trash, and ultimately the environment.

But Cayce went beyond these simple physical principles to include our *thoughts* in this equation. He reminded us that "thoughts are things" and that everything we think has either a positive or a negative influence upon the outer world—impacting others as well as the overall environment. Science has also given several demonstrations that there is an environment of thoughts, sometimes called the "field of consciousness."

The "Global Consciousness Project," for example, studies the effects of world events that grip global awareness on radioactive devices. These devices, housed in numerous laboratories around the world, have previously demonstrated their sensitivity to consciousness effects. When events such as the death of Princess Diana or the 9/11 World Trade Center destruction grip the awareness of the world, these devices respond to the effective force of having so many people's awareness focused in the same manner. Clearly Cayce was correct when he said that our thoughts become part of the environment we all live in. Such a realization begins to put upon us a tremendous responsibility for how we think. Just as we might cover our cough in public so as to not spread germs, we might consider cleaning up our fear and anger thoughts so that they will not "pollute" or harm the world. Developing ourselves spiritually, so that we have more constructive responses to the events in life, is what we need to do individually as our own part in cleaning up the "thought environment."

It becomes apparent fairly quickly that the concept of oneness takes on many dimensions, and begins to reshape our view of the world, of our lives, of how we are connected to one another, and of how we may need to address some of our response patterns. Cayce often pointed out to inquirers that the reality of oneness could not help but characterize their experience of the world. On the one hand, he noted the oneness of soul, mind, and body, whereby the shape, functionality, and experiences of the body ultimately mirrored that of the soul. Along the same lines, researchers of reincarnation have often noted bodily marks that correspond with recalled incidents from past lives. For example, a traumatic injury in one life, such as a critical wound, can result in a mirrored-image "birthmark" in the next. Another indication of oneness is reflected in Cayce's oft-repeated quote, "Spirit is the Life, Mind is the Builder, and the Physical is the result." This certainly illustrates the Cayce view of personal creation—essentially a downward causation model in which attributes of the soul are mirrored and represented in the mind, which in turn is mirrored in the physical conditions that are eventually created.

An even more profound dimension of this oneness within a person is the oneness between the person and his or her life experiences. Frequently, an individual would approach Cayce and inquire about the meaning or purpose of a specific life circumstance only to learn that the situation was a lesson that somehow provided a mirror of that person, and her or his attitudes, beliefs, and actions. Sometimes this oneness is expressed by the slogan, "You create your own reality." We can take this on the micro level, meaning that the "you" (your ego, your choices), makes a difference in the world. At a more macro level, however, what Cayce means is that the external "movie" that you call "life" mirrors an internal "movie"—the two are one and the same.

While we are desperately aware of our life's circumstances, we are more often ignorant or unconscious of the deeper aspects of ourselves that become projected and reflected in our life's events. We can see the result, but not the cause, and it was the cause that often lay at the heart of Cayce's explanations. Every one of our life's experiences is like a personal mirror that invites us to learn more about our relationship to All-That-Is, or Reality, or God—for ultimately oneness demands that *God is all there is*. Our life's experiences are reflections of our soul—mirrors that we can learn from in the same way that we can learn from our dreams. Our experiences reflect who we are. Our spiritual path moves us from perceiving ourselves to be as our ego experiences us—as separate, autonomous individuals. Yet life is attempting to teach us a different consciousness of reality: Although we are individual, we are one with All-That-Is; we are one with God.

As a personal example of trying to apply Oneness, Travis was a twenty-year-old college student who had decided to try to work with this concept for a week by "seeing the light of God in everyone I contacted." His approach was to simply look at people directly when he passed them, smile, and in his mind think the words: "I salute the light of God in you." Several days into the exercise, he had an experience.

Travis was standing in a hallway at school waiting for a class to end before he could enter the room. While waiting, he made a point of looking at everyone who passed him in the hallway and practicing his oneness exercise, when something suddenly happened: "All at once it was like I was connected to everyone! As someone walked down the hall toward me, and I looked at them, suddenly it was like I was looking out through that person's eyes, and I could even feel that person's footsteps walking through the hallway. I felt as though everyone was a part of me and somehow I was a part of everyone. The thought came to me, 'I wonder if this is how God sees us?' And as soon as I had a thought, the experience was gone." Travis became convinced that he had personally experienced Oneness.

Achieving this shift in perspective and perception requires using more of our consciousness than simply our mind or head consciousness. It requires "heart," as Cayce notes, as the purpose of our heart awareness is to allow us to conceive of ourselves, and directly experience ourselves to be individual, yet one with God.

We can actually see this parallel in science. Destroying the illusion of separation between observer and the external world, the science of atomic physics discovered that "the observer affects the observed." Later on, quantum physics discovered that the "things" that we assumed were the building blocks of the universe—electrons—were not really things (little separate particles) unless you observed them in a certain manner. Otherwise these "things" were really waves that spread infinitely outward, with no boundary or set location. Here we see the notion of two realities: one kind of perception sees the world of bounded, separate things, while another kind of perception sees the world as interacting waves of vibrations, a cosmic dance of not "things" but expressions of energy. Edgar Cayce made a similar distinction, noting that the reality that we perceive with the senses is not the only reality. He advised us to learn to see with the soul mind, which uses the imagination or the realm of the heart.

Just as your heart can feel "close" to someone far away, science has discovered "non-locality." When electron pairs in a molecule are separated from one another and propelled quickly in opposite directions, they nevertheless react instantaneously to each other's actions. Even though they are far apart, what scientists do to one also affects the other at the same moment, no matter how far apart the two electrons may have traveled. Science has discovered what they call a "non-local" effect, something that scientists of consciousness find quite similar to a psychic effect. There is no separation by distance or time. In a very radical statement, Cayce described space and time as illusions that enable us to experience cause and effect and ultimately learn from that experience. In other words, God created these illusions in consciousness to provide us an opportunity to move from the perception of separation to the consciousness of oneness. Science is catching up.

People often link Cayce to the concept of a New Age because of his prediction of the transformation of our worldview, primarily that of moving into a consciousness of Oneness. Years ago, when Marilyn Ferguson published her groundbreaking book, *The Aquarian Conspiracy*, outlining the various aspects of the emerging "Aquarian Age," she focused on one central idea that she felt was the cornerstone of all the changes coming. She called the old "paradigm"—meaning the worldview that governs the questions we ask and the answers we get—the worldview of separation. She claimed that the notion of separation was dying, and in its place was the idea of inter-connectedness. Thus the idea of oneness is the core idea, and our questions may be shifted from asking, "How does it work?" to instead asking things like, "What is the story?" This would be a shift from the materialistic thought-pattern of cause and effect, to the more consciousness-oriented concern for meaning and purpose.

When Cayce was asked by people going through trials and tribulations about what was the meaning of all their suffering, his answer was consistently provocative as it expressed a radical view of oneness, but one which gives us a handle on dealing with our predicaments. He echoed what is known as the "Perennial Philosophy," the key idea central to all spiritual traditions. In simplest terms, the philosophy states, "you are that!" This mysterious statement is saying that the outside world that you experience and the inner world that you identify as being you are actually one and the same. The outer world is our mirror. The meaning of this mirror, and Cayce would suggest that it is its purpose, is to awaken us to our God-ness. Every experience we have, Cayce contends, is meant to lead us to the realization that we are one with God; that we possess the attributes of godliness, especially in our creative aspects. As we develop spiritually, grooming our thoughts and behaviors to express more perfectly our ideals—as we aim less to get ahead in the world, but instead to become in harmony with the world—we find it easier to learn from our experiences, to grow from them, to realize that everything is God, and everything exists to wake us up to our own God-ness. Everything that exists and all that can be conceived to exist is One. It is all ONE.

3

Finding Companionship
with the Creator

WHEN THE 19TH CENTURY PHILOSOPHER NIETZSCHE WROTE THE
words, "God is dead," it was to present his premise that the world no
longer saw belief in a higher power as the ultimate stage of wisdom and
enlightenment. By the turn of the 21st century, however, God was no
longer "dead," but instead many new books appeared bringing God to
life in surprising new ways. New viewpoints, merging the paradoxical
findings from quantum physics with modern studies of the transpersonal nature of the human mind, have proposed an intimate connection
between God and consciousness itself. These new viewpoints mark a
trend to bring God down from the sky and into our hearts, transforming
God from simply a distant fatherly figure into a core creative element
seeking awareness and expression within each human being.

Although he used conventional biblical language, Edgar Cayce's
viewpoint on God anticipated this profound development in our image
of the Creator. He provided a unique rationale that allows us to engage
in our own personal exploration of the meaning of this reality in our
lives. There is a purpose, he contends, for why God created us in the
first place. That purpose is the key to our experiencing the truth behind

a great mystery: God created us, according to the Cayce readings, for the purpose of companionship.

When Edgar Cayce was asked to describe whether God was a loving parental figure or an impersonal force, his response was that both answers were correct. Cayce also made the surprising assertion that rather than being apart and separate from humankind, ultimately God's desire was to bring an awareness of the divine into physicality and the third dimension through each of us. Hidden in the implications of what Cayce proposed is a much more radical theology involving the Creator's actual need for us in the continuing development of creation. The idea of "companionship with the Creator" doesn't seem like a radical idea, because the warmth of the image deflects us from contemplating such perplexing questions as: Why would God, Whom we believe to be Total, Omniscient, and All Powerful, need our companionship? What could we mere mortal humans possibly add to God? What would our companionship contribute to God?

While writing the "Philosophy" chapter of Cayce's biography, *There Is a River*, author Thomas Sugrue asked a series of questions in a reading about the nature of God and God's purpose in creating humankind. The response given was that God might best be described in terms of oneness and love, and that souls had been created out of God's desire for companionship. What this suggests is that the nature of God is ultimately connectivity with the rest of His creation, and connectivity and love can only be experienced in relationship to other beings.

Consider your own experiences with companionship. When you go on a trip, for example, what does having a companion accompany you add to your experience? Oftentimes, there is something about "sharing" an experience with another person that enhances it. When our companion reflects our observations with statements like, "Yes, I see what you mean," our subjective impression receives an objective confirmation. Having our experience mirrored back to us has an important effect—it makes it more real! A mirror, both in our lives and in mythology, has very special powers to add something to our experience of ourselves.

Have you ever sat and watched an animal in front of a mirror? What makes it so fascinating is our realization that the animal might recognize its reflection. We know from our own experience that looking into a mirror gives us an experience of ourselves from an outward, objective viewpoint. Consciousness studies suggest that we are like animals who are unwittingly confronting a mirror. We know now that we live in a "virtual reality," as if to confirm the ancient Hindu notion of "maya," that we live in the illusion of a dream. Our experience of what we think of as external reality is actually a mirrored reflection of our true identity as events in consciousness. This distinction between the "objective reality out there" and the "subjective reality inside our heads" has implications for our relationship to the Creator.

Following Cayce's recommendation for comparative study, when a group of students of the Cayce readings toured Japan, they were invited to a Shinto shrine, a holy place of the Japanese indigenous spirituality. In the shrine, in a prominent position on the front wall, in the same place that a Christian church might display a cross, there was a large mirror. The Shinto priest stated that the mirror was their sacred object and only initiates were allowed to look into it directly. For that reason, the priest turned the mirror slightly aside. Whereas for Christianity, the coming together of God and man can be symbolized in the cross, for the Shinto, the mirror expressed this same possibility.

Perhaps the biggest conceptual drawback we have to understanding our true companionship with the Creator is that we too readily identify with our physical nature rather than with our spiritual reality. From the standpoint of the Cayce readings, we are not physical bodies with souls, but spiritual beings who happen to be having a physical experience. The problem is not one of trying to become something else; rather, it is one of not living up to the very best we already have within us. We are already spiritual beings! The truth of our divine nature is clearly illustrated in this popular Hindu legend:

At one time, all people on earth were gods, but they so sinned and abused the divine that Brahma, the god of all gods, decided that the godhead should be taken away from them and hid in some place where humanity would never again find and abuse it. "We will bury it deep in the earth," said the other gods. "No," said Brahma, "because they will dig down in the earth and find it." "Then we will sink it in the deepest ocean," the gods said. "No," said Brahma, "because they will learn to dive and find it there, too." "We will hide it on the top of the highest mountain," the gods said. "No," said Brahma, "because they will someday climb every mountain on earth and again capture the godhead." "Then we do not know where to hide it where it cannot be found," said the lesser gods. "I will tell you," said Brahma. "Hide it down inside the hearts of the people themselves. They will never think to look there."

The Cayce material confirms the fact that we have forgotten our true nature as children of God. Instead, we have so identified with our physical lives and our earthly experiences that we no longer remember why we came into the earth in the first place. Simply stated, our goal is to somehow bring heaven into the earth. Many individuals have incorrectly assumed that the goal is to get out of the earth, and have even stated things like: "I hope this is my last life. I just want to go to heaven and rest." Yet, this is looking at our heritage from a perspective quite different from that contained in the Cayce information. In fact, the readings confirm that God desires to be expressed in the world through us—with the example set by Jesus being the pattern for every soul.

What may come as a surprise to even students of the Edgar Cayce material is how an individual's soul growth and one's ability to become cognizant of a connection to the Creator are intertwined. In some respects, this awareness is defined in Cayce's spiritual growth material as the lesson on "Cooperation." But rather than being a lesson on how to get along with others, Cayce's premise is that the lesson is ultimately about learning to cooperate with God so that the divine can work through us. The reality of being companions and co-creators with God is a reality for the present, not something that becomes true upon physical death or when a soul achieves enlightenment or reaches heaven. The challenge, in part, is overcoming the perception of our separation from the Creator.

The Cayce readings give pointers regarding our separation from God and the path to return to the desired state of companionship. An easy way to gain some experience that may lead to a better understanding of this process is to turn your attention to your breathing. Stop reading for just a moment, and focus on your breathing for perhaps a dozen breaths. When you've taken a moment to focus on your breaths, you can continue reading.

Based upon reports from countless people, when you turned your attention to your breathing, you probably began to adjust it in some manner. It's almost automatic for us to take control of our breathing as soon as we pay attention to it. But before you turned your focus to your breathing, it was happening on its own, naturally. You were, so to speak, unconsciously "one" with your breathing. But as soon as you paid attention to it, you experienced your breathing as something that you observed, separate from you, and you began to control it. Here the "ego" stepped in to assert itself (e.g., "You're not breathing deeply enough") and created a separation from the natural state of breathing. Just as your breathing was an effortless expression of your nature before you paid attention to it, once you did, you turned breathing into your "job."

To experience what it might be like to drop this sense of separation, and become, once again, one with your breathing, but conscious of that oneness, pay attention to your breathing while letting it be. Explore the affirmation, "I am aware of my breathing, and I let it be. I let go and let Spirit breathe me." Here you can learn, in a simple situation, what Cayce meant by "watch yourself go by" while acknowledging and trusting in the guiding presence of a greater wisdom. It is a relaxed, receptive stance of the ego; the ego is not eliminated, but it becomes a witness to the activity of the Creative Life Force within the temple of the body.

Edgar Cayce asserts that each soul has within itself the seed of awareness of and companionship with the Creator. Modern research in comparative mythology and dream symbolism has demonstrated that the human unconscious mind does contain a buried notion of God. What happened to it? In describing the "Fall," Cayce makes a distinction between our sensory mind and our soul mind, and how that affects the aspect of God we can experience. When we look at the world with our senses, we experience ourselves as separate from the world out there. The senses allow us to experience the impersonal side of God, the physical universe that scientists can observe and study. How do we perceive with the soul mind? It is through the imagination. Often we express this process when we say that we can "see with our heart" what is invisible to the eye. As Cayce put it, "the purpose of the heart is to know yourself to be yourself and yet One with God." (281-37) Thus we experience the personal side of God internally, intuitively. And what is the personal? It is that which has the experience of "I AM." Perhaps you recall that famous expression coming directly from God's lips: "I am that I am." It means that God defines Himself as that reality that is the source of the primal, universal experience of being, the "I am" experience. Our intuition hints that there is a point of conjunction where we meet God. It is within the heart of our own "I am" awareness.

The most frequent opportunity to experience the blessing of this connection is probably the most important. It is when we interact with others! Becoming aware that the "I am" experience within us is identical to the "I am" experience within others provides the link for this connection. Become aware of it, realize it, honor it. The Creator within each and every person awaits your recognition, your companionship. The word "Namaste," which in Sanskrit literally means "I bow to you," is used as a greeting throughout Asia today. Buddhists say to each other, "Namaste," meaning, "The Buddha in me greets the Buddha in you." Just as the "I am" reality is the same for us all, we all also desire happiness. Just as you have needs, so does the other person. Kindness and compassion for others is a natural result of these realizations.

The Cayce material expresses a similar sentiment. When we gratefully offer our presence to another person, when we are willing to share the moment, listen, acknowledge, and affirm the presence of the other person, we are on the threshold of Heaven. From the Cayce perspective, Heaven is not somewhere we go alone as we achieve righteousness but an experience we share with others as we honor and serve the Creator within us all. If the Creator desires our companionship, then we offer it best when we offer it to one another. We may serve others in a variety of ways, but to offer companionship is to serve the awareness of the "I am" that unites us. To do so is to acknowledge the presence of the Creator in our midst, which is the companionship the Creator ultimately desires.

4

All of Life Is Purposeful

OVER THE FORTY-THREE YEARS THAT HE GAVE READINGS AND HELP to people from all walks of life, Cayce frequently counseled individuals facing every manner of hardship, heartache, and loss that, with time, their experience could be seen by them as purposeful. In other words, somehow the challenge could potentially be used to be of assistance to the individual having the experience and possibly to others as well. One of the more all-inclusive hypotheses put forward by the Cayce readings is that all of life is purposeful. To be sure, sometimes seeing the purpose in something takes a skill beyond sensory observation. It requires a change in consciousness; it can require seeing beyond the physical self; and, it often involves the intuitive imagination. To accept that there is purpose to life also requires acknowledging a reality beyond the domain of waking consciousness and personal ego. In practice, exploring Cayce's premise of the purposefulness of life relies upon perceiving subtle truths, and exploring the hidden key to life that the Cayce information postulates for all of humankind.

Let's begin with a simple analogy. Suppose we present a group of scientists from another planet with one of our automobiles. Being alien to our world, they do not know what this object is, but they begin to investigate it with their research tools. They measure its length, width, and height, and take measurements of each piece they can isolate on this large "contraption." They take as many observations as possible, keeping careful records. They discover that pushing a round thing labeled "ignition," causes many of the parts to begin moving and making noise. They see gray vapor coming out of a tube at one end. Someone discovers that if you press on a lever down below the sound increases, the speed of movement of the parts increases, and the gray vapor is replaced by a blast of hot smelly air coming out fast!

And so it goes. There are so many measurements these scientists can make. But what are they discovering? If they did not know the purpose of the object—to convey folks to distant locations—how would they know how to make relevant measurements (horsepower, fuel economy, braking distance, handling, etc.)? Taking a friend on a moonlit drive, the thrill of navigating a curvy mountain road—these and other pleasures of driving remain unknown to the alien scientists unless they discover the purpose of the automobile.

How many of us on earth have ever made the appropriate measurements of the human being? Have we even asked the right questions? Collectively, we've certainly accumulated enough observations, and we've proposed many theories. Evolution is a theory based on many observations of nature. The idea of "cause and effect" is a meta-theory, a universally applied assumption about how the world "works," which is to see all living processes as functioning like a machine. Another term for this worldview is "the clockwork universe." More recent advances in science have introduced the mysterious "uncertainty principle," concerning the unpredictability of the moment and direction of the "quantum leap." Cayce's own vision of "God" displays both of these properties—the ironclad chain of cause and effect that describes God like electricity—a force that acts upon the physical world; and the highly personal "I am" that is within each of us as our awareness and capacity for free choice, which becomes more and more unpredictable the less we are driven by the cause-and-effect force of determinism.

Ultimately, the Cayce information suggests that the "why" of life is to encounter a series of experiences that will ultimately awaken each of us as individuals to an awareness of our true divine self. Somehow, collectively, we have forgotten the truth of our divine origins and the fact that we were created—as Cayce puts it—to become "companions and co-creators" with God. From this premise, all of our life experiences (both challenging and wonderful) and each of our relationships (also challenging and wonderful) have the potential to expand our limited consciousness beyond the ego self.

Just as Cayce asked the question as to the "Why?" of life, for thousands of years countless stories and myths have arisen in respond to humanity's asking "Why?" Their existence demonstrates our tremendous need for an answer to this question; a question to which science alone may not be able to provide a response.

What is it about humankind that we wish to know our meaning, our purpose? Where did we get that quality of curiosity, and how does it play into creation? To answer these questions, we need to look at the ways in which humankind has responded to the need to find meaning and purpose through myths. What are myths? One could say that myths are stories about our origins and its challenges. A myth can sometimes be presented as fictional, and yet in your heart, you know it's true.

In a fashion similar to that provided by Hinduism, Cayce describes the creative principle as awakening from a slumber to begin a cycle of exploring possibilities. Just as a person might paint a picture to make what's inside visible, to gain a sense of self, Cayce's view of the Creator's motivation for creation was for the joy of self-expression and the desire to experience oneself through that expression. Sound familiar? Sound human? Give a kid a crayon and he or she will scribble on the wall, and then look at what was created. The creation of souls was part of God's expression. God expressed Himself as souls. The purpose of that expression, as with any self-expression, was for God to experience Himself through His creations. In the case of souls, God gave souls all of His own qualities so that God could experience the companionship of these souls. The reflection of God that souls provide gives God the desired companionship, and thus the greater self-awareness.

In thousands of readings, Cayce explored the gradual growth in collective humanity's consciousness by examining the mythic tales of Atlantis, Lemuria, Egypt, Persia, Rome, and other ancient civilizations. Told from the perspective of specific individuals and their personal journeys through various lifetimes, these readings portray the fact that a soul "grows" when it explores its own divine consciousness and its relationship with others whereas it "loses" (opportunities and consciousness growth) whenever it focuses only on the physical world and its perception of self alone.

A similar worldview can be gleaned from the Mayan culture and their religion's approach to an understanding of God's desire for companionship and the challenging opportunity it presents us as participants in creation. Their mythology is such that the Mayans claim to be the fourth "people" of the planet. They believe that God destroyed the first three "peoples," because they could not say the prayers correctly. Was God simply being capricious? No. The Mayans believed that God requires reflection and acknowledgement in order to experience His own existence. The purpose of humanity is to allow God to become conscious of Himself. Our willfulness has distracted many of us from this task, but it is this task that makes life truly meaningful.

Most creation myths include a chapter on humanity's "fall from grace." In the Bible, we have the story of the serpent tempting Eve to bite the apple. Cayce's version tells a different story, and helps us realize how we experience the "fall" every day. There are two parts to Cayce's version. The first part has to do with our use of free will to go our own way, rather than the way that aligns with the divine purpose that God intended for us. We get caught up in our creations, our life dramas, our things, and become "willful." The second part has to do with how our willfulness in exploring our abilities in the three–dimensional earth world keeps us hypnotized to the sensory world, rather than to the intuitively given spiritual world. It's the separation two–step: "I can and will." Although definitely agreeing that at one point in the history of the world there was the physical appearance of humankind (the Adam and Eve story), Cayce suggests that the "fall of man" was ultimately a descent in consciousness; however, rather than being a "bad" choice it was part of our evolutionary growth to bring divine consciousness into the physical world.

A summation of Cayce's story of creation is told in the "Philosophy" chapter of *There Is a River*, the Edgar Cayce biography by Thomas Sugrue. Elsewhere, in *Edgar Cayce's Story of the Origin and Destiny of Man*, author Lytle Robinson provides perhaps the most complete summary of the Cayce perspective on these topics. Scholars have shown that Cayce's intuition is as we might expect to echo the oldest of humanity's notions about essential metaphysical truths. He echoes the mystery religions, whose concern is the problem of freeing oneself from the chains of materiality, having sensed a spiritual or non-material dimension of experience, such as in dreams. The question of "why" takes us to the original purpose. Cayce's intuitive view of creation and its purpose gives an important creative role to the human being in the history of creation. At the same time, his version of creation doesn't fail to point to the foibles of humanity that have affected the course of creation's history.

During that same period that Cayce was delving deeply into his intuition into "the Beginning," the Swiss psychiatrist Carl Jung was looking deeply into the human unconscious. His method was to compare the dreams of his patients with the world's mythology. He asked the question, "How did the idea of God enter into the human mind, and with what purpose?" His conclusion was that when someone is born, they arrive with the full instinctive intelligence of the Creator, but soon learn that the social network, upon which the child is totally dependent, does not want a little godling, but requires a well-behaved social citizen. Hearing "no" and being sent to bed with no dinner, getting criticized by the teacher, one's peers, and other setbacks lead a person to suppress more and more of their natural repertoire in favor of socially acceptable and rewarded styles of awareness and being. Such is the source of separation from the Creator, through such judgments and the suppression of life they brought about. Yet Jung found that his patients' dreams suggested that a person get past such judgments in order to discover and have the courage to live out their authentic self. "Whom the gods cannot lead, they drag," was one of his favorite quotes. If we ignore or refuse "the call" to wholeness, Jung observed, then life seems to bring about circumstances to force change. Jung noted that "character is fate," meaning that those who remain unconscious experience that "stuff happens" to affects their life, but those who embrace the creative life force find their destiny in going along willingly with God's will, even when it takes a lot of effort to discern it. He speculated that synchronistic experiences sometimes point the way. Jung called the source of this activity the psyche. He envisioned it as a non-material, but active force in creation, in our experience, and in life's response.

Cayce's intuitive understanding paints a very similar picture. It has a storyline with the same dynamic of an intelligent life force, operating through the Akashic Records, to bring about circumstances that encourage a person to realize, as Cayce would put it, "all we meet is self."

It is the evolutionary purpose of the Akasha to bring about circumstances that will awaken us to our oneness with God. It is up to us to recognize the opportunities in these experiences. It is not to ask, "What is God's purpose here?" as if there was a specific purpose set in stone prior to the event. The purpose is always the same, generally to give us the opportunity to expand in consciousness and become aware of our divinity. Cayce often pointed to Jesus as the role model for how to live that ideal consciousness of oneness, what he calls the "Christ Consciousness," which, simply stated, is "the awareness within each and every one of us of our ultimate Oneness with God."

Jesus does provide an important lesson on how to experience life as purposeful. In doing so, he gives a spiritual correction to our usual interpretation of the metaphysical thought medicine, "You create your own reality." When Jesus and his disciples meet a blind man on the road, the disciples ask Jesus if the man's blindness is the result of the man's own sins or that of his parents. Jesus responds in the negative, dismissing the retro-consciousness of cause and effect, in favor of the proactive perspective of repurposing the circumstance to fulfill an agenda of Jesus's own choosing, thus acknowledging his role in creation. Jesus says that he will dedicate this man's blindness to demonstrating God's healing power. Then Jesus goes on to demonstrate that his own hands and God's healing power are one. When we use the idea, "All you meet is self—you create your own reality," to explain a misfortune, and we understand it in the three-dimensional causal world manner, then we feel guilty for our failure. That is a misuse of the idea. The true healing power of the idea is released when we embrace the event and use it to discover our divinity by our choice of response.

Practically speaking, how are we to use the events in our lives in such a way that we come into consciousness of the purposefulness of life? We might learn how to ask ourselves a question, such as, "What is it that I can learn from this experience?" Or, "How can I use this experience to help someone else?" Another tier might be to even learn how to respond to adversity with a sense of gratitude, "I wonder what the silver lining might be?" Gratitude fosters a sense of abundance, confidence, and curiosity. Gratitude paves the way for experimentation, for ways to create a stepping stone from a stumbling block, for ways to make lemonade from a lemon. It is this tendency to put toward good use the circumstances that come our way, to repurpose adversities into strategies for innovation that reflects our divine spark of creativity. It is a creativity that has an evolutionary basis, a purposefulness that invites our awareness and participation.

Finding out for ourselves how life engages us when we engage it is a significant spiritual milestone. No longer are we separate, having to fight for our own survival. Instead, we experience ourselves as part of a team, a member of the divine network of learners. As we engage life as a purposeful encounter to create consciousness of our divinity, we can rest assured that the divine is helping out!

5

Learning Through Nature

In both the psychic and waking states, Edgar Cayce was a strong proponent of communing with nature. Nature allows us to witness the orderliness of the universe in that we harvest what we plant. It also enables us to experience an aspect of co-creation. The readings contend that nature is an ideal place to learn about God. It is a wonderful school that enables us to learn about ourselves and our connection with the divine, as well as the rest of creation. Cayce believed that personal awakening and consciousness growth occurred when one was close to nature. When once asked how young children might best learn about God, his answer was two simple words: "In nature." On another occasion, he stated that within each blade of grass it was actually possible to see the Creator's love.

Nature is God's handiwork, of course, and we can perhaps perceive the Creator's mind by studying the designs in nature. But there may be more to it than that. Whatever your own experiences in nature, it may not come as a surprise to learn that in surveys concerning spiritual or similar transformational experiences, nature is always the most frequent context for them. Clearly, nature has something special to offer that we don't always encounter in a church or a classroom.

You may be one of those many folks who feel as if they can be in communication with the trees, like Joseph, a man who likes to lean against a pine tree in order to "exchange energy and healing vibrations." When feeling especially troubled, or when seeking inspiration, Joseph explains that he will lean against his favorite pine tree and just begin to meditate or relax. He reports that inevitably he feels better and often has a sense that he has received "guidance" by communing with nature.

Mary is another individual who states that she experiences "feeling connected" whenever she gets to spend some quality time outdoors. She says that after sitting peacefully outside she begins to feel a special resonance, as if she were "vibrating in harmony with the scenery." While taking time to be outdoors, she contends that she often feels the presence of God.

Chances are excellent that when you think of being outside in nature, it makes you feel good. Chances are almost as good that you can probably recall a very special nature experience, one that made a big impact on you. One thing's for sure, since Edgar Cayce's lifetime there has been a lot of research on the value of being in nature or even being exposed to the natural world.

Most of us enjoy a walk through the woods. Turns out, research shows that it's actually therapeutic. In one study, for example, depressed patients were asked to go for a 30-minute walk. One group walked in the woods, while one group walked in the mall. All of those who walked in the woods emerged feeling better about themselves. Among those who walked in the mall, half felt better and a fourth of them felt worse!

Some explain the value of being in nature in terms of fresh air. As it turns out, however, research has shown that you don't have to be out in nature to benefit, just being able to see it makes a difference. In a study involving at-risk young girls living in inner-city Chicago, researchers found that those girls whose homes had a room with a view of greenery had better grades and showed better concentration and less impulsive behavior than did those girls whose homes only had views of other buildings.

Simply looking at pictures of nature can also have a positive impact, changing a person's value system in the moments afterwards. In one study, a group of participants viewed buildings, roads, and other cityscapes, while the other group observed landscapes, lakes, and deserts. Participants afterwards took a questionnaire assessing the importance of four life aspirations: "to be financially successful," "to be admired by many people," "to have deep enduring relationships," and "to work toward the betterment of society." The group examining the nature scenes showed an increase in valuing connections and community, while those observing the man-made environments preferred wealth and fame. In another test, those observing the nature scenes were more likely to share money won from a game than were those who viewed the man-made scenes. The researchers speculated that viewing nature helped each participant connect with his or her "authentic self," whereas the man-made scenes reminded participants of the stresses of modern life.

Cayce would agree with these researchers that nature reflects our "authentic self"—our god-like self—more so than do buildings. It is worth exploring how that reflection process might operate. Modern brain research has discovered what scientists now call "mirror cells" in the brain that automatically function to stimulate an unconscious mimicry of the visual information the brain is processing. Updating in modern brain technology an old concept of "feeling into" or empathy, researchers now believe that there is a built-in mechanism within the brain for mimicry as a means of understanding. It's as if the mirror cells build upon an old kindergarten truism: "It takes one to know one." It's as if the brain works on the principle. "To know something, become it." That's certainly a variation on using imaginative role-playing to become like whatever you wish to understand. Edgar Cayce calls it "attunement." When we make an "attunement" to something we go through a subtle process of mimicry, of imagining that we are like that something or that quality of something.

There are a number of ways of intentionally creating attunement with nature. Research with students of the Cayce material has demonstrated the value of that attunement, and we'll describe some of them here.

Meditation in nature would seem obvious. Letting the mind rest upon an ideal such as "harmony," which is certainly one attribute of nature, would bring the meditator in attunement with a harmonic pattern of the creative forces circulating within the meditator's own body. It would also place the meditator in attunement with the harmonic relations among the living beings in nature. Meditating in nature seems like such a natural thing to do, no explanation is really needed, yet it is good to remind ourselves of the role of ideals and attunement in even the most natural of the methods of communion.

A practice similar to meditation but with more of a focus on gaining insight or inspiration from one's communion with nature begins again with attunement. First consider this general recommendation Cayce once made that suggests various details of a total attunement process: As you walk in nature, listen to the sounds you hear. Imitate these sounds aloud. Gradually cease the outward sounding, but continue imitating the sounds mentally in silence. Imitating the sounds in silence directs your attention more inwardly. Cayce made the surprising assertion that this practice—meditating on your own silent imitation of the sounds in nature—would develop your receptivity to inwardly hearing the "song of the spheres," which is the auditory version of the creative or unseen forces guiding the physical world. Cayce suggested that a high degree of imitation of nature would help facilitate attunement with it and allow an individual to realize deeper experiences of communion. When we apply this idea, we get some very interesting results.

Suppose a person wished to explore the possibility of gaining insight or inspiration from some aspect of nature, such as a tree. Let's describe in detail the process implied in Cayce's suggestions. First, find a tree that attracts you, and become that tree in your imagination. Begin by approaching that tree respectfully—approaching it as a living being puts you into the proper frame of mind. Acknowledge that it is expressing its creative nature with no reservations. Thank it for being willing to share its secrets with you openly. Wouldn't you be more willing to share with someone who approaches you respectfully than one who demands your attention? The Golden Rule applies here, too.

Botanical research has demonstrated that plants have ways of communicating with each other, and indigenous peoples claim that plants talk to them. Prominent American botanist Luther Burbank declared that the way he was able to get plants to grow new features was by his loving communication with them. Edgar Cayce, an avid gardener, also believed that our attitude around plants had an effect on them. He also stated that vegetables grown by a grouchy gardener are hard on our digestion. Better, he said, that the gardener tell jokes in the garden, even if they were dirty jokes, than to grumble and grouse!

Approach the tree with the respect you'd show a learned elder if you were hoping to receive kind and helpful advice. Stand in front of the tree and begin to imagine what it is like to be that tree. Imagine the roots, deep underground, and then the tree itself rising from the earth and growing into the multiple branches upward and outward. Imagine growing leaves. Imagine being a new little leaf, reddish purple in color and changing to green as it matures. Imagine growing a blossom that turns into a fruit. Feel what it is like to draw nutrients from the ground, from the air, and from the sun.

Make your pretending active. As you imagine being the tree, allow your images to work themselves into your body. Mimic the feeling of the tree in the position and movements of your body. Empathize with the creative miracle of the tree; spread your feet apart, feeling the earth feed you. Spread your arms out like branches and feel energy rise up through your feet and out through your outstretched hands. Let your hands circulate in the breeze and your fingers play with sunbeams. Your body, as a tree, moves to the cycle of life—relaxing and dropping leaves in the fall, shrinking during winter, and then experiencing sparks of new life in the spring. As summer brings greater warmth, your leaves radiate, blossoms bloom with wonderful aromas, and your fruit ripens.

As you join your tree in a dance, allow your mood to express itself in sound. Sing the tree's song. It's a matter of improvising in sound to the attunement you feel with the tree. Begin with a quiet hum, as you feel the nutrients rising up your trunk and branches. Begin making an "ahhh" sound as the leaves dance in the sunlight. As you imagine beginning to blossom, a smile may accompany the sounds of "ahhh." Give yourself over to the spirit of life flowing in the tree, and express that life in your own way—openly, fully. It's a feeling of quiet exuberance, yet charged with energy.

Now sit quietly with your tree. Just be there with it in the experience of your communion. As you do so, recall the purpose for your visit to the tree. Was there a concern? A question? Listen now, and you will feel, or hear, or otherwise sense the tree's response. It may come as thoughts you find yourself thinking, memories you find yourself exploring, or a daydream that takes you on a journey of discovery. Don't be surprised if you hear the tree talking!

When Judith tried this experiment, she was concerned about some of her personal failings. She shared with the tree her sense of frustrations over her lack of perfection. She found the tree responding to her notion of perfection. After she had made her attunement, she sat with her back against the tree and rested. Soon she was involved in a Disneyesque type of daydream in which the tree had a face and talked to her. The tree pointed out several places where events had wounded the tree in various ways. The tree showed her where it had continued to grow through these wounds, healing them and moving onward. Although there were scars, they formed part of the natural beauty of the tree. More importantly, the tree showed her how both it and she were still full of creative juices. She saw that she, too, was still growing forward, and her wounding experiences were adding to her wisdom. She was still "perfect" but in a way she had not seen before, because she had based her opinion of perfection upon her expectations and external measures rather than upon the spiritual essence of her being. The tree set her straight.

Talking to trees, communicating with animals, perceiving the unseen forces of creation—all of these activities rely upon a measure of intuition, and the Cayce material on working with intuition and intuitive guidance apply here as well. An aspect of intuition that is very important in communing with nature is the imagination. Traditional psychologists know that being in nature excites the imagination, especially of children. What psychology is only recently including in its study, however, is something that is implicit in the Cayce material concerning the imagination—it can serve as a channel of perception of those dynamics in nature that are invisible to the eye: the "unseen," the "creative," and the "imaginative" forces Cayce describes as being the behind-the-scenes shaper of what manifests physically—the stuff that we can see with our eyes.

When communing with nature from the heart, feeling the oneness with all life, people are discovering that they become aware of dynamic activity around them. Some, like Edgar Cayce as a child, perceive the "elementals" that are the spirits of plants. Others may perceive the energy of the creative forces pulsing through and around the trees. One may go on "journeys" with animals. When such a special moment of communion happens spontaneously, amazing us with the seemingly magical appearance of things normally unseen, it is easy to focus on this special phenomenon. In the idealism of the Cayce readings, however, it would be a waste to merely marvel at our perceptions. It is more important to realize that these perceptions arise from our essential unity with nature. Whether these magical perceptions arise spontaneously or come from a dedication to developing the art of deep attunement, Cayce would render them of little use spiritually unless these moments inspire in us a renewed respect for nature. He would echo the prayers of native peoples who affirm that nature is like a mother to us and that we need to serve her with gratitude and respect for all that she provides.

Communing with nature for no other reason than to share the love of the Creator is perhaps the best reason of all.

6

Working with Ideals:
Your Creative Spiritual Partner

THE CAYCE MATERIAL IS A STRONG PROPONENT OF THREE TOOLS FOR personal spiritual growth and transformation: ideals, attunement, and application. Of these three, ideals are the most imperative; in fact, Cayce once told a 40-year-old clerk that the "most important" thing that any of us could undertake was to know (and work with) our spiritual ideal. This individual had come to Cayce seeking advice on her health, her work, her home life, and her general welfare. Cayce's response was that if she would focus first on her ideal, many of these questions would be answered in the process. Since the readings indicate that ideals are a central component of everything we do—from making everyday decisions to our personal spiritual growth—it's important for us to understand exactly what ideals are and how we might work with them in our daily life.

One illustrative example can be seen in the story of Rosalind, who was faced with a personal dilemma. She had been out shopping one day when she saw her best friend, Joanne, kissing a man (who was not her husband) in what appeared to be a romantic embrace. Joanne did not see her, so Rosalind continued on her way, but she could not get the image out of her mind. Although Rosalind was aware that Joanne was a bit unhappy in her marriage, she had not thought that things had gone this far. Instead, she felt a bit guilty for having seen Joanne and suddenly knowing her secret. But why did she feel guilty? Rosalind herself had done nothing wrong.

Rosalind realized that she was assuming the worst of Joanne—judging her without knowing the facts. Was she angry at Joanne? Perhaps she should just let Joanne know that her secret was witnessed, and then perhaps Joanne would explain everything. Would Joanne want to know that her secret had been witnessed? How could Rosalind be the best friend possible to Joanne in this situation? She wanted to be loving. Would it be the loving thing to let Joanne know her friend had been seen her kissing this guy? But if Rosalind mentioned the incident, what would be her real intention in informing Joanne of such? Would she just be trying to force Joanne into sharing something she had not previously chosen to share? What was the loving thing to do in this situation?

Rosalind had to reach down into her deepest values and intentions in order to resolve the troubling situation. The more she thought about it, the more she realized that if she were in Joanne's place, she would want her friend to be more understanding and to have more compassion. In the end, Rosalind chose to remain silent and focus on being more compassionate, rather than choosing the "tough love" approach she had contemplated. Therefore, Rosalind meditated on the feeling of compassion. She found herself being more at peace with herself. She came to realize that having loving compassion for her friend was a much higher ideal than trying to discover what was going on in the situation. In her mind, she surrounded Joanne with love. As she did so, she found that she had feelings of acceptance, understanding, and empathy for Joanne, even though Rosalind didn't know the actual facts of the situation. That was okay by her. She found the path of peace out of her dilemma, and kept her friend quietly embraced in the back of her mind.

About a week later, Joanne contacted Rosalind and asked her to lunch. After the meal and catching up on each other's news, Joanne indicated that she had something special to tell Rosalind, introducing it by saying, "I just knew, Rosalind, that I could share this with you, and you wouldn't judge me, but would help me see my situation more clearly." As Joanne spoke and told the story of her new relationship, Rosalind realized she had made the right decision and really was Joanne's best friend.

All of us have faced dilemmas where there was an upside and a downside to whichever choice was made. No wonder making these types of decisions can be one of our most disliked and challenging things to do. We are free to make choices, but whatever we choose will have consequences. The choice of any action is followed by a reaction. Our freedom to choose, our ability to make choices, and our inability to avoid our choices having consequences are all part of our co-creative relationship with the life force, or God. The best course of action available to us is to make good choices, but what makes our choices good?

In order to make choices, we need to know our values. Often we need to know our highest or ultimate value, what Edgar Cayce would refer to as our "ideal." It's for good reason that he reminds us that becoming aware of our operative values and then consciously choosing our ideal among them is the most important spiritual act we make in our lifetime. On one occasion, Cayce explained to a man that the reason he had so many problems and so much confusion in his own life was because he had never really established a conscious ideal. He often felt like he was in a state of confusion simply because the ideal he had established (unconsciously, to be sure) was that of a "wanderer." He was encouraged to make a conscious choice and to begin to work with it, because whatever an individual dwells upon, they become.

How do you become aware of your highest values and, ultimately, the spiritual ideals that can best become a part of your life's motivation? One way is to begin to imagine the scenario of an ideal day, and then examine that day for the values that it contains. For example, Richard was a self-employed handyman, a jack of all trades, an artist. He was relatively happy, unless he began to compare his modest circumstances to others he knew with bigger homes, newer cars, and exciting vacations. He felt guilty that he hadn't used his talents enough to create as prosperous a life as others. When he was asked to imagine his ideal day, he responded as follows:

"Every morning when I wake up, it feels like Saturday. I have a creative project that I love working on. Sometime during the day, I help somebody with something. At night, I enjoy myself with friends." Examining the values underlying this scenario, Richard realized that freedom of expression was paramount, for the feeling he associated with Saturday mornings was "freedom." There was also the happiness of being engaged in creative pursuits and the freedom to do so. There was the desire to be helpful to others as he was needed. There was the valuing of close relationships and the freedom to be himself among friends. When Richard realized that he actually valued freedom of expression more than the freedom to buy whatever he wanted, he became more at peace with his modest material existence. Having to trade in free time to work more hours to pay for more things than he really needed was not something he valued. In the end, Richard listed his underlying values as being freedom of expression, creativity, and relationships. In terms of his spiritual ideal, he chose service to others. As we become more aware of the existence and functioning of values and ideals, we can take a proactive approach to them.

Since choosing a spiritual ideal is the most important thing we can do, it may be helpful to understand how to identify a genuine ideal. In a purely philosophical sense, an ideal is a representation of perfection that may be beyond us in the present but is something we strive toward. For example, a circle, defined as all points equally distant from a center, exists perfectly only in mathematics. In real life, all circles only approximate the perfection of the ideal. Similarly, in our desire to invent the "perfect mousetrap," it is the perfect that is the ideal which cannot be obtained, while any given mousetrap is a valid representative of the idea of a mousetrap. Pursuing an idea of happiness ("a happy marriage and a fulfilling career") is different from living according to an ideal of happiness ("loving deeply, serving widely"). The first envisions a goal—a concrete, fixed end point. Whereas a goal is something attainable, in Cayce's terminology, an ideal is really a motivating pattern that guides our lives. With a goal, there is no happiness until it is reached, while sometime afterwards the goal that was once so attractive loses its appeal. On the other hand, an ideal is never truly achieved. There is always room for improvement. The ideal motivates us to reach beyond our present grasp. With ideals, it's the trying, not the fulfillment, that is the purpose.

When you can appreciate the spiritual creative power of an ideal, then you are ready to work with it as a purposeful map of the way you wish to live. Here we draw upon Cayce's insight into the channel of creation, or the method by which energy is guided to produce manifestations. The "formula" he gave for it is, "Spirit is the life, mind is the builder, and the physical is the result." Spirit is energy, while the mind patterns that energy to channel the manifested result. Here is how we can assemble the creative power of an ideal. Suppose you wish to grow into the ideal of "being in harmony with all life." Begin to imagine how living according to that ideal would affect your attitude and behavior in various areas of your life. For example, how might this ideal affect us when at home with the family? What mental attitude toward home and family would naturally result from the spirit of harmony? Perhaps it would engender an attentive attitude of receptivity. And what types of behaviors might such an attitude generate? Careful listening and cooperation might be some ways to express the attitude of attentive receptivity. So there's one example of completing the formula: the ideal of harmony at home inspires the attitude of attentive receptivity, which generates the behaviors of careful listening and cooperation. This same process can then be applied to the various areas of one's life.

As another example, let's imagine that I wanted to pick a spiritual ideal that embodied becoming more loving. I might visualize the most loving person I could ever think of—perhaps a spiritual figure like Mother Teresa, or Jesus, or Buddha, or an enlightened Being. I can imagine how it might feel to be around this Being, and even how this Being might interact with others. What kinds of thoughts would this Loving Being hold in mind? What might this Loving Being do if he or she was faced with the challenging situation or problem that I am dealing with right now? What affirmations or meditation verses would a Loving Being focus upon? As I imagine how an individual who embodies my spiritual ideal would respond to life, and I begin acting in that same manner, I am truly choosing and working with a spiritual ideal.

One practical approach suggested by the Cayce material for exploring your ideals is to create a chart. Take a piece of paper and draw three columns. Label the first column, "My spiritual ideal." Label the middle column, "My mental attitudes," and label the third, "My physical activities." Using a previous example, if your spiritual ideal was "harmony" then what attitudes could you hold in mind that might best exemplify harmony? Certainly, harmony would be one, compassion might be another, understanding a third, personal surrender another, love another, and perhaps also oneness. The key is then to pick activities you can do for yourself and others that equate to each of the attitudes on your chart. For example, for the attitude of oneness, you might choose (for self) meditating on oneness. Conversely, for the attitude of understanding, you might choose trying to discover all of the things you have in common with someone with whom you are having challenges. Ultimately, you bring the spiritual ideal into manifestation by choosing attitudes and activities that can practice that ideal in daily life. For each person in your life, for each circumstance you face, you can create a row in your ideals chart to indicate as your ideal the spirit in which you wish to meet that area of life, the attitude such an ideal implies, and the desired behavior you plan to follow—behaviors for self and behaviors in response to others.

Creating an ideals chart not only is valuable because of the thoughtful work it requires, but also because it can become an object of contemplation. Repeatedly, the Cayce readings emphasized the power of the mind in creating the substance of an individual's life. The oft-repeated quote, "Mind is the Builder" is especially important in working with ideals. You can readily survey the life you are building for yourself by the ideals you hold and the attitudes and behaviors they generate. Along the same lines, you can come to understand the type of person you are (and the life you are creating) in the process of becoming cognizant of the ideals that inspire you, the attitudes that are empowered by your ideals and your values, and the actions and activities that fill your day's events. Taken together, it becomes clear why setting a spiritual ideal is the most important tool for growth and transformation that we have at our disposal.

7

Reincarnation and Everyday Life

THE EDGAR CAYCE READINGS PRESENT THE UNIQUE PREMISE THAT THE principal purpose for life in the earth is to bring spirit into the third dimension. Rather than escaping the earth, our job is to collectively bring divinity into the physical dimension. On a personal level, that goal is accomplished by undergoing a series of lifetimes in which each person eventually awakens to the individuality of the soul-self, comes to recognize the spirit within, and ultimately manifests unconditional love and enlightenment—just as the Creator intended. The universal laws of reincarnation and karma are the process through which each of us are able to experience "cause and effect" and the ramifications of each of our choices until the soul realizes that ultimately its desire is simply to manifest the soul's oneness with God. From the premise of the Cayce material rather than being a "belief," reincarnation is instead a verifiable process that enables the soul to come to know its true self and its ultimate relationship with God.

This ultimate journey toward enlightenment, growth, and individuality is detailed in countless examples of archetypal myth and literature. As these myths go, there is often the cyclical theme of an original paradise, a separation from that paradise, an ensuing struggle in a challenging world, and finally, having experienced a personal transformation, there is a return to paradise in a new consciousness. The biblical story parallels this cycle. Adam and Eve are in the Garden of Eden. They eat of the forbidden Tree of Good and Evil and are expelled from paradise. The struggle of humanity ensues until the advent of Jesus and the offer of a Kingdom of Heaven within, which is a reward for a rebirth wherein a person is transformed from a physical to a spiritual being.

Rather than coming to a full understanding of the purpose of reincarnation, too many individuals believe that the ultimate goal of being in the earth is simply to get to heaven. However, if getting to heaven were the ultimate goal, why would an all-loving Creator bestow upon each individual life experiences that are very different from one another? Why would God give one person a life of plenty and personal opportunity and another a life filled with loss, sickness, poverty, hunger, or all manner of tragedy? Wouldn't this worldview suggest that the Creator may not be as all-Loving and Compassionate as we might hope? Also, if heaven were the only goal, doesn't it suggest that physical incarnation is ultimately irrelevant? The answer from Cayce's perspective is that life in the earth is purposeful, that each of us has been sent to the earth as an emissary of the divine—ultimately bringing spirit into the earth—and that even the most challenging experiences are chosen by the soul as a means of eventually helping others with the very same experience—essentially becoming a "Christ" to someone in need. In the same manner children learn through experience and by facing the consequences of their choices and actions, the soul undertakes life's lessons as a means of gaining experience, awareness, and personal wholeness.

Sometimes the events of our lives entail challenges and experiences that force us to draw upon resources we did not know we possessed. Sometimes we struggle with these challenges and lessons until we finally engage the soul's inner wholeness. And as our wholeness is manifested in the earth, we grow closer to the true divine being that we are. The adversities we face are often lessons that enable us to break free of our personal limitations into the glory of our spiritual selves. It is a process that can take many, many lifetimes.

As much as we might like to imagine a world without adversities, these "negatives" play an important role in both general and personal history. The Cayce material consistently rejects the idea of "evil" as a separate force. There is only one force, Spirit, which is God in its active role. On the one hand, the readings present the "fallen angels" as those divine beings who volunteered to follow after humankind as individuals made choices apart from their divine heritage. Cayce also presents the premise that sometimes even a bad choice can eventually lead to a growth in awareness. One oft-repeated quote from the readings is to "do something, even if it is wrong," as the universe can work with our erroneous choices and expand our conscious awareness; whereas idleness or the lack of choice essentially cripples soul growth.

To realize the inherent problems of a world without adversity, imagine a twist on the Jack and the Beanstalk fairy tale, a twist that promotes the "everything is as it should be" paradigm. As the story goes, Mom sends Jack to the marketplace with the family cow to trade for needed food. When Jack returns from the market, he has no food, but instead three beans. We know how Jack's mom reacts in the original story: she gets angry and throws the beans out the window. But in our "everything is as it should be" variation of the story, Jack's mom reacts very differently. She praises Jack! "Oh Jack, you are such a clever boy! Who would ever have thought to trade our cow in for three beans? You are a genius!" Jack smiles, of course, very happy and contented with his mom's praise. Jack's mother continues in her praise with a grand gesture: "Jack, we are so proud of you, that we are going to place these three beans on the mantelpiece so that they can remain as a testimony to your trading genius!" At this announcement, Jack literally beams with pride. As Jack's mom places the beans on the mantelpiece, where they forever remain as a tribute to Jack, his potential as a giant slayer fades away, and his future is assured now as a "bean counter." By sparing Jack the humiliation and pain of knowing he made a horrible trade, she also cheats Jack out of his opportunity to grow beyond being a "mama's boy" as he becomes a man.

Oftentimes when the subject of reincarnation comes up, people ask the question, "Why don't I remember my past lives?" The truth of the matter is that countless individuals have been able to become consciously aware of their own past lives, and all individuals actually do remember on an unconscious level. Books like Carol Bowman's *Children's Past Lives*, Brian Weiss's *Only Love Is Real*, and Roger Woolger's *Other Lives*,

Other Selves, as well as decades of research by experts, including Dr. Ian Stevenson (author of *Twenty Cases Suggestive of Reincarnation*) just to name a few, all confirm that people from all walks of life, cultures, and religious backgrounds have been able to discover the realities of reincarnation and karma. The Cayce readings also contend that as individuals undergo personal transformation and subsequent soul development, they remember past lives, past relationships, and past actions, as a means of furthering growth, consciousness, and understanding.

The use of the will plays an important role in life, because each individual is a complex combination of positive traits as well as negative patterns that potentially come into play in every experience and every relationship encounter. All individuals have the capacity to choose to manifest the very best they have within themselves, or the very worst.

A therapist tells the story of a young woman artist who was experiencing depression and was unable to paint. She had an irrational obsession with the health of her mother, for whom she felt unreasonably responsible. Digging into the source of her depression revealed a past life as a male artist so obsessed with art that he had neglected his wife and child to the detriment of their health and well-being. In that lifetime, as he focused exclusively on finishing what he considered an important painting, his baby got sick and died, and then his wife deserted him. In an act of extreme despondency, he committed suicide by hanging. This memory captured the pain and depression that the woman had been experiencing in the present. She also seemed to transfer her past guilt about the baby's mother onto her mother of this lifetime. She began to experience the obstruction of her artwork as a defense against getting overly involved in it to the detriment of her social and family responsibilities. As she worked through these feelings, she was able to form a conscious ideal of balancing work and family and in the process find creativity in both art and relationships.

In terms of an unconscious awareness of reincarnation, each individual's biases, talents, fears, expectations, and thoughts and opinions of other cultures, races, religions, and time periods in history, often have roots in unconscious memories of past-life experiences. Rather than beginning each life as a blank slate, an individual enters each lifetime with these unconscious memories that essentially remain as a residue from previous actions, experiences, thoughts, and relationships. If this were not the case, we would expect to find that individuals raised in the same families, who attended the same schools, had the same upbringing, and experienced the same formative years might be very similar to one another; however, anyone with siblings can easily attest to the differences that exist between brothers and sisters. Heredity and environment can help to explain the similarities we have with family members, whereas the soul's individual journey through time and history can explain the differences.

It is important to point out that the purpose of understanding reincarnation is not to begin compiling a possible listing of former incarnations and time periods but instead to use that past as a learning experience in the present. In fact, Cayce told one individual, " . . . to find that ye only lived, died and were buried under the cherry tree in Grandmother's garden does not make thee one whit better neighbor, citizen, mother or father! But to know that ye spoke unkindly and suffered for it, and in the present may correct it by being righteous—that is worthwhile!" (5753-2) In other words, ultimately the purpose of coming to an understanding of reincarnation in our personal lives is not about the past but is about what we are doing in the present and the future we are building for ourselves and our world.

A prominent teacher used to tell the story of how he had become aware of one past-life experience as a ruler, someone who had responsibility for a great number of people during a time of dangerous upheaval and change. During that lifetime, he had been subject to a number of expectations that got in the way of what he was convinced was best for his people. In fact, he found the role of ruler constrained his freedom of action and creativity. At the end of that life, he had died very much frustrated that he had not been able to bring about his grand vision for his people. Perhaps because of that frustration, in this life he felt that the leadership experience was more of something to overcome than to build upon. Instead, he acknowledged that what he had decided to "learn" from that previous experience was to be more open to the many possibilities that enabled him to serve others, especially ways that encouraged and allowed individuals to make their own choices. He truly became much more open to doing things other than "his way." He became much more sensitive to the needs of others, and he became interested in helping individuals find their own power and leadership. Ultimately, he came to believe that his awareness of the past was instrumental in enabling him to help others, as well as finding greater balance and wholeness within himself.

In Cayce's worldview, the inevitable destiny of every soul is to become cognizant of one's true individuality while maintaining an awareness of our oneness with God. For all of humankind, this state of enlightenment is seemingly achievable in one of two ways: either by learning the lesson of love and then moving on to other stages of consciousness development or by literally attaining perfection in the earth. Of the thousands of individuals who received readings from Edgar Cayce, less than 20 were told that they had so mastered the lesson of love that another earthly incarnation would not be necessary unless they chose to return. Apparently, there were "many mansions" in which they could continue their individual growth process. In terms of manifesting perfection in the earth, the example repeatedly cited by the readings was that of Jesus. Apparently, Jesus so mastered the earth curriculum as to become an Elder brother for every soul regardless of his or her religious background or belief.

The Edgar Cayce readings see reincarnation as the means for assisting each and every soul in consciousness and enlightenment. Ultimately, that growth is about bringing spirit into the third-dimension. In fact, that is essentially the reason each and every one of us is here—to bring the divinity into the earth. From Cayce's perspective, reincarnation is not really about trying to discover who we were and what we were doing in the past—the past is instructive only in what it can bring to our growth in the present. Instead, we are challenged to focus on the here and now, dealing with those relationships, lessons, struggles, challenges (and joys, blessings, and opportunities) that will enable us to become all that we were meant to be: divine beings having a physical experience in a limited dimension of consciousness.

8

Relationships, Families, and Soul Mates

WE LONG FOR CONNECTIONS WITH OTHER PEOPLE. IT IS THE SOUL'S quest for wholeness that intertwines us with all kinds of personal relationships, whether they are physical, emotional, or spiritual. We have relationships with family members, with the people we work with, and with others in our communities. Relationships arise through all the activities and interests with which we are involved. The soul uses these relationships and interactions with other people for a very important purpose. It is here that we encounter our own frailties and weaknesses—those things that we need to work on. It is through our experiences with others that we also come to know our strengths and what we have to share in terms of offering another support, encouragement, and nurturing. It is through a lifetime of encounters with all kinds of people—at home, at work, and in the world at large—that we truly come to know ourselves, and to know the truth of our identity as spiritual beings sharing our lives with others.

The family and all the personalities within that family are the first group of relationships that we experience. As if in preparation for other areas of life, the family life often involves relationships that are chal-

lenging and perhaps even harsh, but generally also entails relationships that are positive and nurturing. These conditions do not arise
by accident. In the Cayce material, there is a repeated reference to the
spiritual axiom that everything happens for a purpose. With regard to
relationships specifically, souls prepare their incarnation by choosing
their parents and other significant persons with the purpose of gaining
needed learning experiences. As with other soul intentions, our conscious, thinking self finds it challenging to consider such possibilities.
Of course, if it weren't a challenge, there wouldn't be any growth potential in it. We can experience some of that growth simply by opening
our minds to the expanded view of relationships that the Edgar Cayce
material offers for our consideration.

Our lives are journeys in the growth of consciousness. As souls, our
awareness may be unlimited, but when we incarnate into materiality,
our physical brains dominate and limit our consciousness. It is as if we
have to do our earth learning from scratch, in the school of hard knocks,
gaining from experience. Edgar Cayce's understanding of the mechanics
of learning about ourselves through interactions with others anticipated modern psychology's understanding of "projection," the process
whereby we encounter our unconscious qualities by experiencing them
in other people. Other people, particularly, and most of our experiences generally, serve as a mirror for us to perceive ourselves. In other
words, what we often experience and encounter is actually a reflection
of ourselves, and not an objective imprint of the outer world. As kids
we teased, "It takes one to know one!" expressing an instinctive understanding of this principle. Edgar Cayce was fond of quoting the biblical
version, "And why beholdest thou the mote that is in thy brother's eye,
but considerest not the beam that is in thine own eye?" (Matthew 7:3)
Psychologists understand that we bring our unconscious mental sets to
organizing our perceptions, thereby unwittingly revealing ourselves in
the form of our understandings. As it says in the Talmud, "We do not
perceive the world as it is, but as we are."

From Edgar Cayce's perspective, someone who truly inspires and
uplifts us can also provide us with a mirror of our own potentials and
possibilities—perhaps even the very things we possess that could inspire others. Conversely, the very things that challenge and irritate us
about another person are generally a reflection of the very things we

need to work on within ourselves. Every relationship has the potential to assist the individual in becoming a better person—we planned it that way! Although at first we might be repelled by this idea, have you ever stopped to wonder why someone you are challenged by has a best friend? Or, why your own best friend may have someone who does not like him or her? The reason is because each of us sees something very different in another person and that "something" is generally a reflection of ourselves. If you want to see what deficiencies you need to work on spiritually, look around at the people in your life that irritate you. If you want to see what resources you have to help you grow and serve, look around at the people that you really love and admire. The perspective of the Cayce material casts a new light on relationships and what we might seek from them.

As we grow up, we are often conditioned to believe that the purpose of relationships is for our own personal satisfaction. Fairy tales, romance novels, and the movies portray love in such a way that we develop unrealistic expectations. We search for relationships that will make us happy. Our own natural longing to be loved influences our search for meaningful experiences with others. These inner promptings to find wholeness and fulfillment outside of one's own self are at the heart of the misperception that a loving relationship with another person is the key to happiness. It is ironic that many individuals spend a lifetime looking for that perfect someone to make them happy, all the while unaware that the soul's need for interactions with others is what will help them to become whole within themselves, and thus able to experience happiness, within or outside of a relationship.

Rather than thinking that only upbeat or fulfilling relationships are positive in nature, the Edgar Cayce information contends that even the most challenging of personal encounters can be beneficial. We learn from such struggles. Unfortunately, however, too often people see challenging relationships as something to be avoided. It is also misleading to believe that an unhappy relationship is "karmic" and needs to be endured as some kind of never-ending punishment or lesson. Neither the avoidant nor the submissively resigned approach is helpful. Instead, what is called for is a change in consciousness, understanding, and behavior. It is like a recurring nightmare that cries out for the dreamer to learn a new response to a tired situation. The Cayce perspective insists that the purpose of life's difficulties is not to punish but to evoke previously unrealized personal resources and stimulate learning new responses.

Here's an interesting story that illustrates this idea. A corporate executive supervised a departmental manager who was overbearing and demeaning to his own staff. Although this manager's professional background was impressive, his demeanor toward subordinates was unacceptable. The executive dismissed that manager, and wanting to avoid a similar mistake at all costs, the executive went through an extensive search process, ultimately hiring a woman with an equally impressive background. All was fine for about three months until the executive realized that the new manager was becoming "overbearing and demeaning" to her staff, just as her predecessor had been! The executive was stunned at this development, and began to reflect upon, "How could this have happened?" Much reflection yielded the insight that all the employees reporting to the new manager had one thing in common: each was somewhat introverted and appeared self-doubtful, perhaps even to the point of possessing low self-esteem. The executive suspected that it was these employees' need to learn to speak up for themselves, and the manager's need to learn how to deal with subordinates who possessed low self-assurance, that had created this recurring situation. The executive then found a helpful way to communicate this information to all involved. What followed was a change in consciousness that resulted in a major change in the workplace atmosphere.

All relationships involve work of some sort—patience, cooperation, and an openness to change. Looking for an easy "soul mate relationship" may be an illusory and self-defeating goal. When individuals came to Edgar Cayce and asked about a soul mate, he generally responded that a "soul mate" was an individual with whom someone had a strong emotional connection (positive or negative) and that the connection continually brought the same individuals back together again to learn from one another. In other words, a soul mate is an individual to whom we are drawn in the present, because we have been together in the past. It is a relationship in which each individual has the opportunity to be of invaluable assistance to the other's personal growth. This concept of soul mates is quite different from that proposed by contemporary society. In fact, a web search of the term "soul mates" will return millions of sites, most of which buy into the idealized version of soul mates first proposed by Plato (ca. 427–347 BC), who suggested that humans are forever looking for their counterpart, because they were once divided in half by Zeus. The division of humankind into its male/female counterparts is actually an archetypal story that exists in every religious tradition. Yet the archetype is ultimately about the soul's quest for personal wholeness instead of a mirror image of oneself. Rather than being limited to romantic relationships, each of us possesses all kinds of soul mate relationships. These relationships manifest within families, among friends with whom there is a deep bond and connection, with individuals we are drawn to and yet challenged by, and even in work relationships in which individuals are brought together to achieve some common goal.

Oftentimes, Cayce encouraged individuals to assume responsibility for creating the type of relationships they would ultimately like to have. He encouraged people who wanted to experience more love in life to be more loving. He encouraged someone who wanted to have more friends to be friendlier. He counseled an individual who sought to be better understood by others to be more understanding of others. On one occasion, a husband complained to Edgar Cayce that his relationship with his wife was less than ideal. He asked the sleeping Cayce how he could encourage his wife to be a better wife for him. Cayce's advice was simple: He encouraged the husband to compile a list of all of those qualities that he thought his wife would list as being desirable in an ideal husband. Cayce instructed the husband that he should use that list as a set of directions for how he could become his wife's ideal husband. If he did so, Cayce affirmed, in time he would find himself married to an ideal wife!

The question often arises as to how to differentiate between a potential long-term relationship and one in which there is simply an attraction in order to work through something from the past. Cayce suggested that true love was ultimately best expressed as "giving in action," where one was not concerned with what was received in return. Whereas desire is a feeling or a condition in which an individual wants to draw someone to him- or herself, true love is an expression of emotion, energy, or activity that goes out to others without thought of self in return. In addition, Cayce also suggested that long-term commitments with individuals were best undertaken when two people worked together with a common ideal, and for a united purpose. In other words, "What are we hoping to accomplish by being together?"

To be sure, the readings were not goody-goody in suggesting that every relationship could become "ideal." In fact, on a number of occasions Cayce counseled individuals with advice that, for their own physical, mental, or spiritual safety, they needed to leave a relationship. On a few occasions, he counseled couples that they had learned their respective lessons and that their usefulness to one another was over. For the most part, however, he encouraged individuals to understand that most relationships have the potential to be a purposeful and a helpful experience in terms of soul growth and personal transformation. By being with these individuals, we are somehow provided with an impetus to become a little more whole within ourselves. This idea that all of our relationships can ultimately be a helpful experience is very different from what most of us have assumed. Our relationships grow to become what we make of them. We might ask ourselves questions like the following: How can this relationship make me a better person? How does this relationship challenge and stretch me? How does this relationship encourage me to become more balanced? And even, What is my soul trying to learn from this relationship?

At the heart of the Cayce information on relationships, families, and soul mates is the idea that through an ongoing process of interactions with others, the soul finds itself involved in a curriculum of personal growth and development. Ultimately, this curriculum is designed with our own growth and wholeness in mind. It is through our relationships with others that we truly come to know ourselves.

9

Karma as Memory

WHAT IS KARMA? ALTHOUGH A FREQUENT TOPIC OF DISCUSSION, IT IS without a doubt one of the most misunderstood subjects dealing with the journey of the soul. Even enthusiasts of the Edgar Cayce information often share mistaken assumptions about what karma is, the ways it impacts the soul's journey, how it interacts with free will, and what it means to us in relation to other individuals. Too often the subject of karma has created an impression of disempowerment and futility in regards to experiences that are presented to the soul—that somehow this is "my karma," and there is nothing I can do about it. In actual fact, however, the Cayce readings provide a unique look at karma that is both helpful and empowering. From this approach, karma is neither a debt nor a limitation but is instead an energized soul memory activated within the individual. Moreover, this memory is just as likely to be helpful and beneficial as it is to be challenging and detrimental.

On one occasion, a twenty-seven-year-old woman asked Edgar Cayce for information about what "karmic debt" existed between herself and a member of her family. In response, Cayce told her that she, like many individuals, misunderstood the karmic principle. Rather than something burdensome, scary, and inevitable that existed between herself and another person, the reading encouraged her to view karma as simply a personal memory that she had to deal with. Furthermore, her karmic memory of the relationship she had once encountered with this particular family member was very likely to be very different than the memory the other individual possessed about that very same past-life experience. Rather than being some kind of debt or tie between her and her relative, in reality the karma in her experience was simply a memory to which she had some kind of personal attachment. To be sure, it was a memory that the woman had to work through, but the memory was hers alone. Perhaps what is most instructive to personal understanding is the readings' assertion that her present life experience had brought this same individual to her again as a means of working through her own past-life memory. Her karma was simply her unconsciousness attachment to the memory of the relationship she had once encountered. Cayce told her that there was no such thing as a karmic debt between people; instead, there were only personal karmic memories in relationship to others.

For clarity, let's examine two different individuals and their differing approaches to personal karmic memory—one helpful and one perhaps less constructive.

In terms of working with karmic memory from a more helpful perspective, Hugh Lynn Cayce (Edgar Cayce's eldest son) often shared his experiences working through a lot of difficult karma with his own father. From Hugh Lynn's perspective, one of his most challenging karmic memories had been created during a period when he and his father had both been in positions of authority in ancient Egypt. In addition to vying for the people's favor, during that period they had also both fallen in love with the same woman. In part out of jealousy, and in part out of politics, during that lifetime Hugh Lynn eventually managed to banish Edgar Cayce from the country, effectively ending Cayce's influence upon the people for a time.

In this incarnation, Hugh Lynn came into the earth effectively choosing one of his former rivals as his own father. He had to work through his personal memories of jealousy and competition. On one occasion, when talking about his experience with this karmic memory, Hugh Lynn offered the following: "I had a rough time with Edgar Cayce. For me, he was far more than just a father (a very good one), far more than just a good Sunday school teacher, far more than the greatest psychic I've ever seen come down the tracks . . . He was many other things, too, that I had to face and deal with. And yet, fortunately, he was also the most loving person I've ever known. And it was beautiful to deal with my jealousy and my hate, which I had at that time, in the light of his love that he was able to transmit. It was a beautiful experience, and it worked out. I've cleaned up a lot of stuff." In Hugh Lynn's experience, he spent his entire life becoming the strongest supporter, advocate, and promoter of the Edgar Cayce work—effectively transforming his previous memory of what had once transpired between them with this new experience.

A less productive approach to karma is illustrated by the typical misunderstanding in the life of Pauline. She described her lifelong issue with personal "karma" by noting how, throughout her life, she experienced repeated criticism and felt constantly undermined by comments of some of those closest to her. She described her father as being extremely critical and verbally abusive as she was growing up. In order to escape a disastrous home life, she married young and soon found herself with a verbally abusive husband. He constantly criticized her and frequently commented that he should have never married her. As her children grew, so did Pauline's frustration level, because she often experienced them as being disrespectful toward her. As a working mother, Pauline now finds herself in an unappreciated clerical position where her boss "often finds occasion to criticize me in front of the other employees." With a sigh, Pauline adds that she feels all of this is "just her karma."

Obviously, Pauline seems to be viewing karma as something she must endure and just accept. However, the way in which she describes her life story suggests that the issue is ultimately about her own feelings of personal self-worth and self-esteem. Contrary to Pauline's assumption about karma, the life events she's experiencing are not intended as a punishing lesson, forcing her to endure humiliating rebukes; instead, the perspective of the Cayce material suggests that Pauline is repeatedly encountering the very same experience until she makes a change within herself! This perspective finds a parallel, by the way, in modern therapy for recurrent nightmares, which are now treated as a developmental blockage. Here the working assumption is that the person experiences repeated dreamtime exposures to a threatening situation in an attempt to stimulate an alternative, more constructive response from the dreamer. When therapy finally inspires such a shift in the patient's awareness of response alternatives, the nightmare ceases. Applying that thinking to Pauline's "karmic situation," the challenge she faces lies not in what other people say to her, but instead in transforming what she thinks of herself! Upon questioning, Pauline admits that she has very little self-worth. Perhaps Pauline initiated this self-esteem issue by extreme self-criticism in a past life, and her "karma" is ultimately to face and overcome her own personal criticism. As all our life experiences are purposeful, hers seem designed to enable her to finally work through her negative thoughts about herself. Once Pauline is able to do this, she will ultimately no longer perceive herself as being surrounded by individuals who seem to think as little of her as she does.

Cayce once gave an analogy to explain how karma might best be understood. He stated that it was very similar to the body's own assimilation process. In the same way that the body takes in food, then breaks it down for assimilation, giving the body either strength or discomfort, the soul body assimilates karmic memories by the current life experiences it draws to the person.

In the case of positive karma, these memories come to the forefront as life experiences and stimulate the reawakening of these assets. Examples would include resuming a positive relationship with a loved one and the rebirth of personal talents and aptitudes the soul self has formerly mastered. Cayce frequently described an individual's past life talents and abilities and discussed how those abilities came back to us in the present. In other words, if a person had a talent with music, or child-rearing, or communication, or the law, or government, or compassion—regardless of what that talent or ability was—those skills remained evident in the present as part of the soul's awareness. From this premise, the stories of child prodigies suddenly make sense! It's not that any individual somehow appears in life with extreme talents that are impossible to understand; instead, we take our talents and abilities with us. According to Edgar Cayce's readings on himself, it was actually this aspect of positive karmic memory that had enabled him to be born with such a heightened sense of psychic ability—it was something he had worked with, developed, and ultimately, mastered in the past.

Negative karmic memory can include such things as unresolved anger, biases, animosities, addictions, and other unresolved attachments that prevent the soul from experiencing wholeness within itself. These memories must be faced and resolved, essentially creating a change in consciousness or an expanded personal awareness. For example, the memory of addictive patterns might be reawakened with the very first cigarette or the very first glass of beer. How the individual deals with that reawakened memory in the present will determine a portion of his or her actual life experience. It is important to point out that even "negative" karmic memories are not inherently bad or good; they are only memories. The dynamics of whether or not the memories lead to more positive or more negative experiences on the soul's learning agenda remain a matter of free will.

In Cayce's own life experience, he stated that the reason he had to go to sleep each and every time he gave a reading was that in a former lifetime he had misused his psychic ability for selfish pursuits. Although the psychic talent remained a part of his soul self, this time around—as a means of overcoming that former selfishness—he had to "set self aside" by going to sleep each and every time he gave a reading.

To be sure, both positive and negative karmic memory can affect relationships and experiences in the present; however, free will remains the strongest component in determining how an individual actually deals with his or her reservoir of memory. In fact, on one occasion Cayce told a forty-seven-year-old woman that ultimately the course of her life experiences would be dependent upon how she utilized her free will in regards to her karmic memory. For each individual, it is actually the attitude and the will that becomes the greatest determinant in an individual's life, rather than karma. It was this dynamic that prompted the Cayce readings to frequently use the phrase that life's experiences could become either stepping-stones or stumbling-blocks depending upon what the individual did with those experiences.

Although it is a subject unto itself, it is important to briefly mention the concept of grace that permeates the Cayce information on soul growth. On one hand, karma can sometimes be equated with the Old Testament equivalent of "an eye for an eye," or the scientific principle that for every action there is an equal and opposite reaction. Without the intended change in consciousness or an expanded personal awareness, the precision of karmic memory can come in to play in a "payback" kind of way. For example, you cheat me out of $10 in this life, and therefore I am going to cheat you out of $10 in the next—just so you'll "know how it feels!" Although that type of exchange certainly expresses the eye-for-an-eye understanding of karma, it is not actually in keeping with karma's principal goal of expanding awareness. The reality of grace is ultimately the possibility of spiritual inspiration—of expanding consciousness without having to undergo actual reciprocating experiences. It is possible to have a change in consciousness and expand personal awareness without confronting in experience the specific consequences of the karmic memory that has been created within the self. That possibility is the operation of grace. In other words, personal attunement and my own growth in consciousness could pull together life experiences that enable me to understand that taking someone's $10 falls short of the mark. Through grace, I could gain that awareness without having to undergo the actual experience. Both karma and grace are vehicles for the expansion of personal consciousness.

Another component of Cayce's unique contribution to better understanding the reservoir of karmic memory is the notion that it is just as easy to reawaken and energize a negative karmic memory as it is a positive one. It is for this very reason that he recommended setting a spiritual ideal. As each individual focuses upon cultivating the very best that she or he possesses within self, negative karmic memory patterns can be eradicated and replaced with more positive approaches that can help to facilitate personal wholeness.

A final example of how karmic memory can unconsciously affect an individual in the present is evidenced in the case of Max and Judy, and their son, Mike. As Max and Judy tell the story, when their son was about one year old, and on approximately a dozen occasions, he would wake in the middle of the night, pull himself up the bars of his crib, and throw himself to the floor—a distance of more than four feet! Once he hit the floor, Mike would begin crying, and Max and Judy, hearing the commotion, would run to his aid. This happened so frequently and without apparent cause that both parents believed their son was either going to break a bone or become seriously injured. Not knowing what else to do, one evening Judy decided to see if she could somehow "tune into" or even "imagine" what it was that her son was experiencing.

As Judy sat in the chair next to her son's crib, the image came to mind that she was in France many hundreds of years ago. (The scene made sense to her, because during her pregnancy she had seen the image of a seventeenth century Frenchman walking out of the nursery.) In her mind's eye, she saw Mike, who was a grown man in the scene, being arrested for something he did not do. Although he repeatedly proclaimed his innocence and put up quite a struggle in the process, he was thrown into a large wooden barred cage and then carted off with horses pulling the wagon. It became instantly clear to Judy that whenever Mike awoke in the middle of the night, he was connecting the bars of his crib with the bars of that long ago cage. When Max heard the story, he took the walls of the crib down and made it into a day bed. The result was that Mike never again threw himself out of bed. Even if the child awoke, he simply stayed in bed and went back to sleep.

Ultimately, we may need to reconsider the definition that has long been applied to the subject of karma. It is not a debt, and it is not a punishment. Karma is simply an interactive, energetic memory that the soul draws upon while dealing with experiences and relationships in the present. Positive karmic memories can be helpful in reawakening personal talents and abilities. Negative karmic memories often call for a change in personal consciousness or an expansion of awareness. Karmic memories can definitely influence and shape our actions and response patterns but only to the extent that we allow them to. Nothing about our lives and our life experience are destined or set in stone. In actuality, life is an unfolding process of growth and development connected to experiences and relationships that are a portion of the soul's ultimate journey toward personal wholeness. Those experiences are not "out to get us" or set in place to somehow punish us, rather they are simply portions of a learning agenda designed to expand the soul's consciousness.

10

Meditation, Prayer, Affirmations, and Attunement

THE EDGAR CAYCE INFORMATION ON MEDITATION, PRAYER affirmations, and attunement has touched the lives of hundreds of thousands of individuals around the world. To be sure, Cayce was one of the first sources in the Western Hemisphere to consistently recommend meditation to individuals from every religious background. The Cayce readings on prayer advance the ecumenical nature of prayer and discuss the workings and vibrations of this integral tool for personal attunement and spiritual healing. In terms of affirmations, the Cayce material frequently extols the extraordinary power of the "mind as the builder" and the premise that personal co-creation is empowered by that which the mind dwells upon. In other words, what one continues to think, one eventually becomes. With all of this in mind, it is ironic that this extremely valuable wealth of information and encouragement grew out of personal failure on the part of Edgar Cayce.

As background information, approximately two-thirds of the Cayce readings deal with health and the treatment of physical illness and disease. Edgar Cayce's lifelong dream was to have a hospital that individuals could come to and receive psychic readings from him, where physicians and healthcare professionals from every discipline and background could carry out the recommended treatments. The readings are a strong proponent of every school of medicine learning how to cooperate and coexist for the ultimate benefit of the patient. For decades, Edgar Cayce sought funding for his hospital before finally receiving support from two New York businessmen, brothers Morton and Edwin Blumenthal, who financed the Edgar Cayce Hospital in Virginia Beach, Virginia (the location recommended by the readings). The hospital opened in 1928, and Cayce's dream became a reality. The dream was short-lived, however, as the hospital was lost in 1931, during the Great Depression. Edgar Cayce was devastated. He was 54 years old, and it appeared that his purpose for living was over.

In response to the hospital's failure, and in an effort to find another focus for Cayce's amazing psychic talent, a group of Cayce's friends rallied around him looking for a way to work with the readings as a group. Some of the individuals were interested in obtaining readings on how they could become more psychic themselves. Others hoped to learn how to become more spiritual, helping their families and the world at large in the process. Edgar Cayce's readings to the group presented the unique idea that psychic development was actually a natural byproduct of spiritual growth and attunement. It was for this reason that the group began receiving a series of readings that promised "light to a waiting world." The group called themselves a "study group," and group members worked for years to compile two books on lessons in spiritual growth that would eventually be published as *A Search for God, books I and II.*

The group activity gave birth to much more than material on soul growth and personal transformation. After the first meeting, Edgar Cayce had a dream that led to the formation of a prayer group made up of some of the original study group members. This group called itself the Glad Helpers Prayer Group—a group whose members were specifically interested in the possibility of raising personal vibration and consciousness as a means of becoming healing channels to others through prayer and spiritual healing. (To learn about the current activity of the Glad Helpers Prayer Group, visit EdgarCayce.org.) Essentially, the readings premise on meditation, prayer, affirmations, and attunement is that as an individual raises his or her personal consciousness, spiritual healing can be directed to others "on the wings of thought." In addition to ongoing meetings, the group would receive sixty-five readings on topics including meditation, prayer, the use of affirmations, consciousness development, vibrations, and even a series of readings on interpreting the Book of Revelation.

Although we may think of prayer as telling God what we need or want, Cayce believed that true prayer was not so much a petition for things as it was an expression of one's desire to gain an awareness of the Creator's will in our lives. In other words, prayer invites God to work through us. Meditation, on the other hand, is clearing aside all random thoughts so that we might become more attuned to the divine. The readings suggested that prayer might best be understood as speaking to the divine, whereas meditation is akin to listening to the divine within.

Although some schools of thought contend that the mind gets in the way of the meditator and must therefore be blanked out, the Cayce information suggests that whatever the mind focuses upon becomes a greater portion of the individual's core: physically, mentally, and spiritually. In fact, when used constructively, the mind is a powerful tool which allows for a greater sense of relaxation and an awareness of the closest possible attunement. For that reason, the readings recommend not to meditate on "nothing," but to instead use affirmations while meditating. These affirmations are essentially encapsulated positive thoughts that the individual wishes to develop within her or his own consciousness. Thoughts such as, "I am at peace" or "I am still and feel the presence of God" could be useful as meditation affirmations. Cayce's approach to meditation also differs from the Eastern method that today we learn as "mindfulness." Although Cayce would respect the ideal behind this approach—in his own words, he recommended learning how to "watch self go by" as an excellent ability to develop. He bases his recommendations for meditation on a different goal: to become a conscious companion with the Creator.

In addition to the importance of the mind's focus, therefore, Cayce also stated that an individual's ideal or intent was extremely important during the practice of meditation. Ultimately, the purpose of meditation should be centered on the concept of learning how to better express divine love in our interactions with one another. Actually, the readings suggested that the entire process of meditation should be taken seriously as it was one of the best vehicles for cultivating our personal relationship with the Creator.

Any individual can take advantage of Cayce's suggested approach to meditation by following a few simple steps. First, get into a comfortable position. It's probably best to sit in a chair, keeping your spine straight, your feet flat on the floor, and your eyes closed. Find a comfortable place for your hands, either in your lap or at your sides. In order to help with a balanced flow of energy throughout the physical body, the readings suggested keeping your palms face down against your legs or closed against your stomach. Slowly take a few deep breaths and begin to relax. Breathe the air deep into your lungs, hold it for a moment, and then slowly breathe it out. With your mind, search your body for any obvious tension or tight muscles. You can try and relieve the tension by deep breathing, imagining the area is relaxed, or by gently massaging any tightness with your fingertips. When you have become comfortable and more at ease than when you first sat down, you are ready to move on. If you wish, the Cayce readings recommended a breathing exercise to assist in even greater levels of relaxation and attunement. Very simply, it is as follows:

First, breathe in slowly through the right nostril (covering the left nostril with your hand and keeping the mouth closed), then pinch your nostrils and breathe out through the mouth. Repeat this for a total of three times. Second, with your mouth closed, slowly breathe in through the left nostril (covering the right), then cover the left and breathe out through the right. Repeat this, as well, for a total of three times.

When your breathing exercise is complete, next, begin to focus your mind on a meditation affirmation or perhaps a single peaceful, calming thought. Instead of thinking about what went on at work, or what has to be accomplished with the remainder of your day, try focusing instead on a thought such as, "I am at peace" or one of the many affirmations suggested by the readings. You can also use a biblical verse (such as the Twenty-Third Psalm or the Lord's Prayer) or a thought with a focus such as, "God is Love." Any of these can be considered an affirmation.

The first stage of meditation involves thinking about the message of your affirmation. In one of the examples cited above, you would think about the words, "I am at peace." After a few moments of thinking the words, you should be able to move onto the second stage of meditation, which is feeling the meaning behind those words. For example, you could continue saying the words, "I am at peace," however, the feeling behind these words can be much more meaningful than the actual words themselves. For an analogy of how a feeling is more all-encompassing than a thought, consider saying the words, "I love my child" versus feeling the meaning behind those words. From Cayce's perspective, whenever individuals are able to hold the feeling of the affirmation throughout their entire being, they are truly meditating and building the focus of the affirmation within themselves.

Sometimes certain physical sensations may occur in meditation: energy rising up the spine, gentle movements of the head and neck in a circular or side-to-side motion, etc. These sensations are simply a result of the movement of energy (often called the "Kundalini" or "spiritual energy") rising through the endocrine centers of your body: gonads, Leydig, adrenals, thymus, thyroid, pineal, and pituitary. If your absorption in the contemplation of your ideal, as expressed in your feeling the heart of your affirmation, is sufficiently meaningful, you might find that you can allow your mouth to form a little smile. If that happens, you will experience and confirm what laboratory research has confirmed—a rush of endorphins!

During meditation, try to hold the feeling of the affirmation in silent attention without needing to repeat the words. Whenever the mind begins to wander, simply bring your focus back to the words of the affirmation. Once again, you would begin by thinking the words of the affirmation and then by trying to concentrate on the feeling behind those words. Don't be discouraged if you find yourself thinking more about distractions than the affirmation—it takes practice. To begin with, you may want to spend anywhere from three minutes to fifteen minutes trying to hold the affirmation silently. Longer meditation periods will become possible with practice and experience.

To close a meditation period, the readings emphasized the importance of consciously sending out prayers and good thoughts to other people and situations in life. At this point, you may wish to open your palms to enable the energy of meditation to flow through them. Since we do not always know what may be best for an individual's personal growth and development, it is best to simply pray that the individual be surrounded by light, love, and God's will, presence, and protection rather than praying for something specific. Studies on the effectiveness of prayer confirm Cayce's recommendation in that groups using a form of general prayer had better outcomes than groups using prayers with specific intentions. It may be that using a general prayer affirms the perfection of God's will, thus aligning the praying person with the beautiful truth. More specific requests express an underlying sense of separation from God, and are thus somewhat self-defeating.

As you begin to practice meditation daily, it will become easier. You might also discover that whatever feeling you have been focusing upon in meditation will actually begin to carry over into greater portions of day-to-day life.

William experienced just that transition. He had recently renewed his commitment to meditation by working with a different ideal and accompanying affirmation. Meditating on enjoying the feeling of being in harmony with God's will, he found it to be particularly peaceful. He was pleasantly surprised that he didn't squirm during meditation or scold himself for not "meditating right." He noticed that he had unconsciously dropped his daily habit of noting telephone calls and other tasks he needed to do each day. Instead, he found he was enjoying going with the flow of his day, trusting he would accomplish his "to do" list, as "edited by God," quite naturally and spontaneously. One of the most concrete effects of this new approach to his day was his ability to contact two hard-to-reach clients. Instead of reaching voice mail when he called them on schedule, he'd call them on the spur of the moment, when he "got the feeling," and would find the client answering the telephone. In many ways, his timing improved to be in more harmony with the way things were. William enjoyed feeling more at ease and natural, with less striving, in both his meditation and in his daily life.

Positive affirmations can also be extremely helpful at working with the readings' concept of "Mind is the builder." For example, someone who is having issues with personal anxiety might find it helpful to create affirmation cards that state things like: "Be still and know that the divine is with you," or simply "Take a breath and relax," or "It is possible to find inner strength within yourself." These cards could be placed around the home, at work, or even upon one's checkbook as a gentle reminder each day of the thoughts that one wishes to create.

Affirmations can be used in a variety of ways.

Through the regular practice of meditation, you can begin to heal yourself on many levels. Developments in the power of brain imagery have led to new significant research on the physical effects of regular meditation. Studies with long-term meditators have revealed that meditation can change both the structure and the functioning of the brain. We know the brain is like a muscle, and it develops with use. One of the brain's muscles that meditation strengthens is the response to emotional stimuli. Long-term meditators can have deeper and more empathic responses to events, even negative ones. Yet their brain returns to peacefulness much more quickly than non-meditators. Meditation seems to enhance a person's resilience.

As you focus upon a positive affirmation, you may find that your negative habit-patterns will begin to change to be more in keeping with your positive affirmation. It is while practicing the silence of meditation, by relaxing your physical body, and by quieting your conscious mind that you can set aside your daily concerns and attempt to attune yourself to your spiritual source. Meditation enables you to be informed by the intelligence of the Creator and the opportunity to consciously serve creation with your unique perspectives and talents.

For decades, individuals from every background and religious tradition have found the Edgar Cayce information on meditation, prayer, and affirmations extremely helpful in their own personal growth and attunement, and personal attunement is at the core of understanding our true spiritual essence. In Cayce's worldview, the end result of soul development is that all individuals will eventually realize their true spiritual self and their connection to the Whole.

11

Understanding Inner and Outer Earth Changes

EVER SINCE IT'S PLANETARY BIRTH, THE EARTH HAS BEEN IN A process of constant and ongoing change. Just as the earth is in a state of never-ending change, so too are our bodies. We are made of the same planetary elements and, in fact, replace all of these bodily elements at least once every seven years—all the while remaining the same person! The physical systems of earth evolved through a chaotic process of destruction and creation, of breaking up and then recreating in a new way. Our cells, made up of planet Earth, reflect that history. Edgar Cayce noted that within each cell, within each atom of each cell, there is consciousness and deep memory. Just as the earth grows through upheavals, so do we as humans. It is in our DNA; it is in our unconscious; it is in our dreams and our myths. Native peoples speak about massive destruction. Their myths echo the theme in the biblical story of Noah's Ark that God sometimes produces these upheavals out of necessity, to clear the way for humanity's evolution toward a more God-pleasing species. At times of great changes in history, it is natural, therefore, for people to be particularly sensitive to changes in the earth, as it strikes a deep chord within—reminding us of the changes potentially we must traverse to reach our ultimate destiny.

During the forty-three years that he gave readings, Edgar Cayce discussed an amazing 10,000 different topics. Whether your interest is acne or Zoroastrianism—or anything in between—there are undoubtedly insights and information contained in the Cayce material regarding your field of inquiry. However, in spite of this immense subject matter, at various times since Cayce's death, the information on "earth changes" has received the greatest amount of attention. Unfortunately, this publicity has prompted many individuals to incorrectly assume that the Cayce material on earth changes could be summarized with such predicted catastrophes as a global future fraught with earthquakes, California sliding off into the ocean (potentially as far east as Nebraska), a shifting of the poles, and a calamitous disaster that would connect the Great Lakes with the Gulf of Mexico and essentially divide what remained of the continental United States into two. These misperceptions present an extremely limited perspective on the true significance of Edgar Cayce's information on inner and outer earth changes. Ultimately, potential geological catastrophes and earthquakes are but the manifestations of a deeper spiritual process involving mankind.

Because of the notoriety of the Cayce material on earth changes, most individuals are extremely surprised to learn that less than twenty readings (out of more than 14,000!) actually address the potential for physical earth changes. Beyond these readings, however, there is a wealth of potentially more important information discussing such things as economic, political, and social changes for the future. There are also readings that discuss the destiny of our collective consciousness as a human family and the strengths and weaknesses of various nations, including their collective lesson as a society. In addition, there is quite a bit of information detailing earth changes in prehistory and the planet's geological past. Finally, there is information in the readings that appears to have been wrong—or at the very least misinterpreted.

The readings that deal with changes in prehistory discuss such things as the origins of creation and the entrance of humankind into the earth. This material includes the topic of Atlantis, as well as brief mention of the civilizations of Lemuria and the Mayans. It also includes information on the appearance of the world's surface in prehistory and how some of that geological surface has changed over time. In addition to discussing hidden archaeological sites and records of forgotten civilizations, Edgar Cayce claimed that the history of humankind went back some ten million years! Although much of this material may be impossible to verify, contemporary research has uncovered evidence to confirm some of the information given in Cayce's trance state. For example, several readings discuss the fact that the Nile had changed its course over eons and had once flowed through the Sahara and emptied into the Atlantic Ocean. These readings found confirmation decades later through satellite imaging technology and on-site archaeological investigations.

Readings dealing with changes for the future offer a discussion of a wide range of topics, including prophecies found in the Great Pyramid and the Book of Revelation. They also include information related to the eventual discovery of records that reportedly were left behind by Atlanteans, a premise that there is a cyclical economic downturn that occurs every twenty to twenty-five years, the possibility of lasting world peace, and information related to the ultimate destiny of human consciousness.

One of the readings dealing with physical earth changes that was obviously wrong (or, at least, mistaken in terms of timing) was a reading given in 1933 when Cayce predicted that a 1936 earthquake in San Francisco would be so catastrophic that the 1906 quake would "be a baby" in comparison. Obviously, such an event did not occur. Other Cayce information that has been misinterpreted includes a dream by Edgar Cayce in which he saw himself born on the coast of Nebraska in 2158, discovering that his work from his lifetime as Edgar Cayce was still being studied. This dream has often been taken out of context by statements such as "Edgar Cayce predicted Nebraska would be the coastline" when, in fact, that is not the case at all. The dream occurred after Edgar Cayce had been arrested for practicing medicine without a license—an event that troubled him greatly. After the dream, a reading was procured and told him that the dream was indicating that regardless of what happened in the external world (e.g., his being arrested), his work was important and would survive—the dream was not about physical earth changes.

Another example of a reading that may have been misinterpreted is one from 1934, in which Cayce asserts: "The greater portion of Japan must go into the sea. The upper portion of Europe will be changed as in the twinkling of an eye." (3976-15) Although interpreted by many as earthquakes, couldn't this statement just as easily suggest the destruction of the empire of Japan and the changing map of Europe, both a result of World War II? Rather than earthquakes or pole shifts, 1936 marked the beginning of civil war in Spain, Hitler invaded the Rhineland in violation of the Treaty of Versailles, and ongoing aggression between Japan and China grew to an all-out war, especially in 1937. Events were set in place causing the outbreak of World War II, and the changes Cayce saw expressed themselves in the affairs of humankind. In fact, in 1935, in response to a question regarding global affairs, Cayce warned a twenty-nine-year-old freight agent of catastrophic events that were building to a world at war that would involve the Austrians, Germans, and Japanese militaries so that the whole world would be "set on fire" by global conflict.

Obviously, the geologic formation of the planet makes some physical earth changes necessary. However, rather than viewing these changes as apocalyptic events, the emerging science of "chaos theory" would view these changes as an ongoing cyclical process of "tearing down to build up better" that continually occurs in nature. For example, even the cataclysmic destruction that occurred with the explosive eruption of Mt. St. Helens led to an amazing rejuvenation process as ash from the explosion supplied minerals that accelerated vegetation growth and diversity. A similar event occurs whenever a lightning strike causes a forest fire that, although devastating at first, leads to the creation of a new forest.

Personal changes can create a similar impetus of growth and change in our lives. For example, oftentimes we hear how a health challenge has led someone to become serious about her or his exercise and diet. Life's challenges can also prompt individuals to draw upon resources they did not know they possessed and transform their lives in an effort to deal with what has been thrust upon them. In order to assist in this process, the Cayce readings stress the ongoing importance of personal attunement, prayer, and meditation, so that we can be led by our own higher resources. At times, we experience the events leading to growth as a major upheaval that feels like the earth has moved. A common example of this kind of inner earth change is someone who has a dream about massive earthquakes only to experience major shakeups in life shortly thereafter.

Sometimes a resistance to taking the responsibility for personal change makes a person especially fascinated by earth changes. Consider this story of a middle-aged man who, in an unhappy job, realized that he wanted to resign but was afraid to do so because of the uncertain future that would result. He noted with fascination all the news reports about various disasters, such as floods, fires, and earthquakes, destroying lives and requiring extreme efforts to rebuild. As he thought about how a flood destroying his home would be a good reason to leave his job and begin a new life, he realized a pattern from his past: he had never quit a job voluntarily, but usually got himself fired, where then he was forced to make the changes he had wanted to make anyway. He realized he had used external crises to get him to move, because of his own fear of taking responsibility for initiating change. He also realized that his fascination with earth changes had a similar motivation: the appeal of having external events forcing him to grow. There was something about this passivity that seemed wrong to him, and he decided to make a change and initiate the process of leaving his job. As he did so, his interest in earth changes disappeared.

The readings would suggest that whatever changes we experience in life as individuals, as a society, or as global citizens is ultimately not about transforming the earth but instead about transforming ourselves. We have collectively lost track of our purpose in the earth, and our evolutionary destiny responds by stimulating awareness. The changing events in our world and in our lives are to enable us to remember why we are here. If our faith is centered on money, then our finances may be tested as we're not in the earth for monetary gain. If we've placed our hopes for the future in political parties or the government, then we can expect political upheavals. If we put our security on our job, then we may need a corporate shake up to help us regain a perspective on what is truly important in life. If we need to come together as a global people, we may need a global catastrophe or calamitous event to bring us together to help one another.

Actually, the readings dealing with changes in world affairs are both insightful and inspiring. These readings suggest that the Christ Spirit actually sat with President Woodrow Wilson as he was proposing the

League of Nations. They are also adamant in their stance that all of humankind must strive to find a common ideal. Regardless of our differences in race, culture, or religion, and regardless of our differing ideas, the readings suggest we can share a common ideal: "'Thou shalt love the Lord Thy God with all thine heart, and thy neighbor as thyself!'"

Elsewhere, the readings suggest that whenever war, strife, and turmoil occur in the affairs of humankind, sun spots occur as a natural consequence. On one occasion, Cayce went so far as to state that the phenomenon of sun spots was inextricably connected to instability and turmoil upon the planet Earth itself. In other words, instability among people leads to instability upon the planet and throughout the universe! Along similar lines, when a forty-year-old woman asked for more information about herself and her relationship to the universe, the response came that for all individuals everything that was out of accord with spirit and divine laws somehow had an impact upon the heavens itself. On another occasion, Cayce told a group: "For as the people of each nation pray, and then live that prayer, so must the Spirit work." (3976-23)

The readings present the premise that whenever we are out of accord (physically, mentally, spiritually, or even globally) with divine law, we bring chaos into our experience. Why? Because chaos can serve the goal of re-introducing creativity into a stagnant situation. Conversely, as we work in compliance with spirit and with one another, we can prompt change in our lives and in our world. In fact, one of the most interesting dynamics of people working together is that they can raise the "vibration" of energy and thought to a higher level. Simply stated, this means that even potential physical earth changes could instead be changes that will occur on a different level. Certainly, some earthquakes will continue to occur as part of the natural physical evolution of the planet. But potentially even more influential changes could come from worldwide political turmoil, global economic challenges, and many more "upheavals" that are not necessarily geological in nature.

In terms of ultimate changes, just what did Edgar Cayce see for our collective future? The readings state that eventually one hallmark of our ultimate destiny could be described simply as "purity." It is important to point out that we're not going to wake up one day soon and think, "Oh wow, we've entered the Age of Purity!" Instead, there is a gradual transition between ages. In addition to purity, the readings suggest that the age we are entering is ultimately one of globalization in terms of understanding that each individual is responsible for every other individual. Certainly, with the globalization of communications brought on by the Internet this may have already become a reality. Finally, in addition to globalization and purity, the Edgar Cayce readings also state that spiritual consciousness will reach such a height of development during this period that eventually each individual will be able to communicate directly with the divine.

In the end, the Edgar Cayce readings on earth changes are really about the fact that a new world is being born. The earth changes we experience—whether geological, economic, global, political, or personal—provide an opportunity to understand our relationship with one another and get our priorities back in focus. These are evolutionary goals that have the Creative Forces behind them as a propelling dynamic.

The time has come to look at Cayce's earth changes material in a new light. The changing events in our world and in our lives are to enable us to remember why we are here. Our planet is in the midst of upheavals that will enable individuals everywhere to eventually gain this realization: with God as our Creator, we are all part of the same family. That understanding and experience is our collective destiny. We don't want to fool ourselves: the geological condition of the planet makes some earth changes inevitable. In other words, there will continue to be earthquakes. But the purpose of the changes we are experiencing is not for the earth changes themselves but simply a step toward reawakening to our joint destiny as spiritual beings manifesting in the earth. We and the earth are as one changing, growing being—a being that is guided by spirit to grow in its awareness of itself and its relationship to creation.

12

The Story of Atlantis

ALTHOUGH THE VAST MAJORITY OF TOPICS CONTAINED WITHIN THE
Cayce material explore practical and researchable topics such as healthcare and wellness, improving personal relationships, transforming
attitudes and emotions, and learning the effectiveness of meditation,
arguably one of the most discussed subject within the readings—for
some it may border on myth and fantasy—is the story of Atlantis. Over
a period of more than twenty years in almost 1,000 different readings,
Edgar Cayce discussed the possibility of a civilization whose technological achievements and accumulation of knowledge rivaled our own.
However, in spite of their collective knowledge, the Atlanteans brought
a series of destructions upon themselves by their misuse of power and
their disregard of divine law—a fate, the readings suggest, that is possible
for every civilization. The story woven together by the Cayce information is essentially gleaned from the personal soul histories of individuals
who had Life readings—those readings dealing with the topic of reincarnation and soul growth—and suggests that records of this mythic
civilization may still be found, proving once and for all that humankind
has inhabited the planet longer than science has yet to understand.

According to the readings, the continent of Atlantis was an enormous land mass situated in the Atlantic Ocean. The first appearance of an Atlantean civilization occurred approximately 200,000 years ago. Because of their quest for knowledge, their ability to build upon the wisdom of others, and their capacity for technological innovation, in time the people of Atlantis advanced far beyond the rest of what were essentially primitive civilizations throughout the world. The readings suggest that the civilization's achievements included a diverse culture, major advances in representative government, a vast system of education, road-building, transportation, renewable energy, major insights into medicine, even flight—and the list goes on and on. Unfortunately, however, these achievements eventually caused some of the Atlanteans to see themselves as just a little better than the rest of humankind. Some of the people of the continent, referred to as automatons, became enslaved, serving in subservient roles to the general populace. Additionally, although for a time the people of the continent had advanced spiritually, many began to lose their direction and sense of purpose by becoming too attached to physicality and the material world. What had once been an almost Utopian society became splintered and lost its way.

The general populace eventually divided themselves into two major factions: the Children of the Law of One and the Sons of Belial. Those numbered among the Law of One carried on the spiritual traditions of their forefathers, remembered their connection to the divine, and at least partially understood their responsibility to those less fortunate than themselves. The second faction called themselves the Sons of Belial. The focus of this group was on the self: self-preservation and the satisfying of personal appetites, greed, and selfishness.

Apparently, the division between the people of the continent was at least partially responsible for a series of three massive destructions that would forever change the continent. The first occurred about 50,000 years ago and came as a result of a massive explosion from their power source; the second occurred about 28,500 years ago, causing the enormous continent to break into three smaller islands; and, the third occurred around 10,500 years ago when the remaining islands sank beneath the surface of the ocean. Prior to the final destruction, there was a massive emigration of the people to various parts of the world, including Egypt, Central America, and Europe. According to Cayce, the only remaining visible evidence of the continent is the Bimini Islands, which had once been a portion of the Atlantean mountain range.

If we ask, "How might Cayce's story of the ancient civilization of Atlantis be relevant to me and my life in the present?" The answer is simply to not forget our connection to Spirit! Obviously, we have to address the demands and challenges of the physical world, but we need to incorporate an ongoing awareness of the ever-present reality of the divine even in the midst of those challenges. It is this very idea that is reflected in the fact that indigenous peoples of America believe that we are in a "fourth world," previous worlds being destroyed by natural disasters created by a God upset with being ignored by humans.

Myth and literature contain many examples of human enterprises or whole cultures that "get too big for their britches" and collapse. In human development, as children mature into adults, they respond to inevitable wounding by developing defensive strategies of survival, accentuating the positive to a fault. At some point in life, events become unworkable given that one-sided orientation, and a "mid-life" crisis brings life to a halt until a new orientation is developed. We often encounter in science, in history, in literature, in mythology, in the Bible, and in the metaphysical writings of other cultures, the idea that "pride goes before a fall," or "developing a virtue to a fault," or "feedback loops in nature create restorative balances when conditions become too extreme." In other words, life often encapsulates an inherent learning process when we forget our spiritual connection or get out of balance in any way.

As a contemporary example of this phenomenon, John grew up a sensitive youngster, often finding his feelings hurt by others. He found that he could "get even" by being the smartest kid. He developed a straight-A lifestyle in school and earned a PhD at a very young age. He received an offer to be a professor at a prestigious university. He was at the top of his game. Only he wasn't. His "drinking habit" had developed into an extreme alcoholic pattern with the result that he trashed his life and lost his academic position. At the bottom of his barrel, he went to Alcoholics Anonymous and learned how he had denied major aspects of his nature, especially his feeling side and his need for relationships with others. Whereas he had developed the defensive attitude that he could "go it alone," the truth of the matter was that John needed other people, and especially needed to be aware of and accept this need. John's "Atlantis" was his intellectual conceit that he was an island unto himself. John is not alone in finding himself going through such an "enantiodromia," or an abrupt change of fortunes and attitude brought about by conditions evolving to extremes.

In the Bible, perhaps the most notable tale of widespread change brought about by destructive human nature is the story of the Flood (Genesis 5-9). According to the story, God eventually became so disgusted with humankind that He flooded the entire planet. Only Noah and his family were found to be worthy enough to survive the Deluge. Noah lived in accord with the divine and, as a result, was provided with instructions on how to create an ark—an ark that enabled him to travel to the new world.

Setting aside how much basis in fact the story may contain (and Edgar Cayce did state that the story was real, although Noah and his family were not the only survivors), there are several interesting points about the ark myth. First of all, it is interesting to note that virtually every culture and continent has its own flood myth. In fact, there are more than 200 flood traditions that are known to exist around the world. Secondly, in most of these accounts—and certainly in the story of Noah—the survivors take with them virtually everything that is a part of their world (e.g., the animals get on the ark). Afterwards, the ark is inundated from above and below with cataclysmic events over which the inhabitants have no control, but in the end they survive, eventually landing on higher ground, and everything that was brought from the old world is incorporated into the new. As an archetypal tale, the story is essentially about being overwhelmed by situations over which individuals have no control, and then learning how to incorporate life's experiences to rise to a new level of understanding—with God and our divine connection as a part of that understanding. Ultimately, the story of Atlantis is about a civilization that had forgotten its spiritual source.

One of the most essential messages in the Cayce material is that each of us has a capacity to find guidance. The source of that guidance lies outside the boundaries of the individual as experienced as separated by sensory-based consciousness. The source of that guidance is the universal intelligence, the Creator intelligence. Its purpose in evolving the consciousness of the human being was to create a means of self-reflection or self-awareness of the Creator intelligence. In other words, God created us so God could become self-aware. When we use our God-given talents, we can be so clever, so ingenious, that we can actually get ourselves into trouble, unless we also maintain a relationship with the Creator. As so many observers today have noted, our advances in technology have far outpaced our moral development.

Beyond Edgar Cayce, there are additional references to this ancient continent. In fact, corresponding to Cayce's timing of the third destruction is the story of Plato's Atlantis mentioned in his dialogues *Critias and Timaeus*. Written in the 4th century BC, Plato tells the story of a massive land and sea empire that had conquered large portions of the African and European continents. However, the continent sank beneath the ocean "in a single day and night of misfortune." According to the tale recorded by Plato, the Atlanteans had mastered ship navigation, making the Atlantic Ocean passable. The continent was beyond the Pillars of Hercules and was larger than Asia and Libya combined. Because of its location in the Atlantic, the story asserts that Atlantis also served as a resting point for excursions to another continent beyond the islands [North America?]. In this version of the story, the destruction was caused by floods and earthquakes so violent that all records of the civilization disappeared beneath the ocean.

In addition to Cayce and Plato, probably the most notable "Atlantologist" was Egerton Sykes (1894–1983). Sykes was the creator of the largest private collection on Atlantis in the world; he was a mythologist, amateur archaeologist, anthropologist, lecturer, writer, and editor who prided himself on knowing every scientist around the world in the field of Atlantology from 1912 to 1950. He took part in dozens of archaeological digs and wrote hundreds of articles. In 1945, Sykes issued a comprehensive "List of Classical Sources," tabulating all of the existing manuscripts pertaining to Atlantis. He also published a revised edition of Ignatius Donnelly's 1882 classic, *Atlantis: The Antediluvian World*. In time, Syke's collection on Atlantis would include more than 6,000 books (in fifteen languages), magazines, pamphlets, photos, slides, tapes, personal letters, unpublished manuscripts, and newspaper clippings. This collection now resides in the library at Edgar Cayce's A.R.E., having been acquired before Sykes' death.

Sykes founded the Atlantis Research Center, an international clear-inghouse for information on Atlantis, and for thirty years, he and his wife published a bimonthly research magazine, *Atlantis*, encouraging scholars worldwide to contribute papers. Sykes proposed that global myths related to an earthly "Paradise" were essentially long-forgot-ten remnants of folk memories related to Atlantis. He was fascinated by similarities among cultures separated by the Atlantic and Pacific Oceans—similarities, he contended, that gave credence to an Atlantean civilization whose destruction had sent citizens (with similar knowledge and ideas) to the four corners of the world. A few examples include the fact that the calendars of ancient Mexico and Egypt were remarkably similar, as was the practice of building pyramids. Mummification was developed simultaneously in Egypt, Chili, Peru, and the Canary Islands. The practice of intentional cranial deformation can be found all over America as well as the Mediterranean Sea. Sykes kept a complete card file index system of these global similarities.

Sykes also theorized that the location of the continent was near the Dolphin Ridge, the backbone of the Atlantic Ridge, in part because a 1936 U.S. Coast and Geodetic Survey of the bottom of the Atlantic indicated that the mid-Atlantic Ridge was possibly once above sea level. Sykes believed that the continent was submerged by a cataclys-mic event, such as an asteroid, leaving survivors on both sides of the Atlantic.

Edgar Cayce's own soul history is also connected to the story of Atlantis in that his readings state that approximately 10,500 years B.C., he was a high priest in Egypt by the name of Ra Ta and had dealings with the people of the continent of Atlantis. During that incarnation, he was instrumental in working with the Atlanteans to preserve a re-cord of their civilization in a yet-to-be-found "Hall of Records" located beneath the Giza Plateau. In addition to the records stored in Egypt, simultaneously records were reportedly stored in the Yucatan and in the mountains of the Atlantean continent.

The Cayce readings predicted that evidence of the lost continent of Atlantis and a record of the Atlantean civilization would eventually be found—spearheading years of sponsored archaeological research in both Egypt and areas around Bimini and the Atlantic Ocean. He also specifically stated on one occasion in 1940 that the first portions of Atlantis would rise again in "sixty-eight and sixty-nine ('68 and '69); not so far away!" (958-3) It was presumed that this meant 1968 and 1969.

Whether or not what occurred was related to Cayce's prediction, it is interesting to note that on September 2, 1968, at a depth of five and a half meters off the northwest coast of North Bimini, three divers encountered what later became known as the "Bimini Road" or the "Bimini Wall"—an underwater formation of rounded stones of various sizes and thicknesses that some claim appear to be man-made. Others suggest they are a natural formation.

As debate about Atlantis continues over whether or not the continent was an actual part of the earth's physical history or just another example of a universal human idea—an archetype concerning the limits of human ingenuity in the context of a larger life intelligence (or both), the readings would encourage us to find that which is applicable in our own lives in the here and now: remembering the importance of spirit as we collectively create the world in which we wish to live.

The story of Atlantis serves as a cautionary tale. It is the nature of humans to inquire into our origins, whether by the archaeology of physical remnants or by the archaeology of images in the human mind. To suspect, or realize, that human history is much greater than the few thousand years explored in our textbooks gives us greater respect for the challenge of evolution and the growth of our own consciousness. We ignore at our peril our inner guidance and our ultimate connection to the divine. In today's changing world, the meaning of spirituality is shifting to mean an allegiance, an honoring of inner guidance, and the respectful and humble application of that guidance toward something higher than self alone. That ever-evolving process is perhaps one of the most essential tools from the Cayce material for creating our new world.

13

Dealing with Fear

DURING HIS FIRST INAUGURAL ADDRESS AT THE HEIGHT OF THE GREAT
Depression, Franklin D. Roosevelt declared, "The only thing we have to
fear is fear itself!" The suggestion was that fear is primarily an internal
issue, not an external one. During the same period in history, Edgar
Cayce was giving readings that stated exactly the same thing about fear.
We have all experienced fear, and it can be anywhere from annoying to
unpleasant to downright paralyzing. Most of the time, it is an invisible
influence functioning as a destructive paradigm that forms our misperceptions, misunderstandings, and maladaptive responses. By distracting
us from our resources, sometimes it can bring about, paradoxically, the
very conditions over which we have worried so much.

The Cayce readings suggest that one of the leading causes of individuals failing to achieve and live out their soul's purpose was fear and not
dealing with longstanding patterns of fear. After studying and working
with his father's material for many years, Hugh Lynn Cayce concluded
that fear was humanity's biggest stumbling block. In his book, *Edgar
Cayce on Overcoming Fear and Anxiety*, he described the main sources of fear
that had prompted individuals to seek his father's help. These sources

were physical conditions, thoughts of death or the unknown, unconscious fears remaining from childhood, fears associated with religion or God, and fears that were connected to past-life experiences.

We distinguish fear from anxiety. Fear is the adrenal fight-or-flight response to the perception of imminent danger. Most of the time, the fears that affect us exist in our minds—a virtual danger rather than a literal one: the anticipation of danger, the possibility of danger, or the conditioned response to past danger. Such manufactured fear is nevertheless an effective disabler. Most fear active in humans today is of this anxious, conditioned sort, as most of us lead lives that are predominately safe from physical harm. Even if it is virtual danger that provokes it, fear is nevertheless a significant inner condition that can prompt both internal and external response patterns.

The best reason to be concerned about fear itself is that it kidnaps our abilities and holds them hostage, disguising its crime with various rationalizations assembled with half-truths. One of the first things we can do in response to fear is begin to recognize if we are coming from a place of fear and then decide what it is we can best do about it.

If you are feeling angry, you are coming from fear. If you find yourself being in a hurry, you are coming from fear. If your friend is talking to you, and instead of listening carefully, you find yourself thinking about what you are going to say in response, deep down you may be motivated by fear. If you are envious of someone's success, there is some underlying fear around that topic. If you are overly obsessive about the pure food you eat, you probably are coming from fear. If it is easy for people to "push your buttons," somewhere there is fear. If you are finding it difficult to be patient about something, fear may be to blame. If you know you shouldn't, but do it anyway, fear may have you hypnotized.

With practice, we can begin to tell when the fear paradigm is active in our thoughts and planning. Begin by exploring the difference in how your body feels when you think "Yes!" in contrast to when you think "No!" Can you tell the difference between how it feels when you have an "open" mind versus a "closed" mind? Explore the difference between seeing the glass as half full in contrast to seeing it as half empty. In each of these contrasts, there is a definite shift in the body sense. It could be the difference between tight and loose, tense and relaxed, or pessimistic and optimistic.

After encountering so many examples of fear in the lives of individuals (as well as in his own life), Hugh Lynn Cayce created a list of eight approaches to working with personal fears, all focused on becoming cognizant of where an individual places her or his mind in the present:

1) Set and work with spiritual ideals.
2) Focus the mind on constructive thoughts.
3) Use the mind to influence the body (and work with the body through relaxation and massage).
4) Cultivate the systematic control of thought.
5) Use inspirational reading.
6) Watch your dreams as a means of observing your real attitude.
7) Use pre-sleep suggestion (or for long-standing fear issues, consider hypnosis).
8) Develop your sense of humor.

The use of ideals is important, because they help to create an ongoing focus for the mind in terms of what the individual is trying to create. Things like, "to become more loving," "to be at peace," "to embody Oneness," and "to be more forgiving" are all examples of possible ideals (more on working with ideals can be found in Chapter 6). The key to working with spiritual ideals is simply to train the mind to focus on attitudes and thoughts that cultivate that spiritual ideal and then to follow through on activities (doing for self and others) those things that will enable you to experience and maintain that positive attitude.

As it relates to overcoming personal fear, Andrew tells the story of being "crippled with anxiety" over the fear of public speaking—a common fear. Unfortunately for Andrew, his occupation eventually required frequent public presentations—at first to small groups of coworkers and then to much larger audiences. In the beginning, Andrew found himself hardly able to speak for ten or fifteen minutes without turning red-faced and stammering. It was only by the repeated use of positive affirmations with himself, "these people want to hear what you have to say," "you know your topic and want to share it with others," "you can easily share the story of this situation," and so forth, that Andrew was able to overcome his fears, eventually becoming a sought-after presenter for his firm.

In terms of constructive thoughts, influencing the body with thought, and controlling thoughts, the readings repeatedly counseled individuals that if they desired to overcome their fears and anxieties, they needed to change their mental attitudes. Many individuals may be aware of a slogan from *A Course in Miracles*: "Love is letting go of fear." The origin is the Biblical verse, "perfect love drives out fear" (John 4:18). The implication is that fear and love are incompatible frames of mind. With this in mind, one possible approach to try when fear arises is to think about something you truly love or truly enjoy doing. What is it that brings a sense of well-being, joy, or fulfillment to you? It is possible to switch from fear to love, and when that happens, many other derivative qualities switch as well. For some, it is a matter of switching from head to heart. For others, it is a matter of switching from a cold, hard heart, to a warm, soft heart.

As we meditate on the bodily felt experience of shifting paradigms of love and fear, we might realize that fear is our response to the perception of separation, while love is the experience of oneness and connection. If you can shift your perspective from separation to oneness or connectedness, you have a chance to shed the fear. In this way, we learn how to recognize fear and use that mindfulness as an opportunity to affirm once again our kinship with the Creator.

In many cases, becoming aware of our fear is not a problem. Instead, the problem is that the fear is so captivating, so hypnotic, so compelling, that it is difficult to break free, no matter how much love and gratitude we use to embrace it. It is when fear is the conscious, formidable challenge that Cayce's recommendations for treatment come into play.

Sometimes fear is a symptom of a physical disturbance, such as an imbalance in the nervous system that keeps the adrenals in a hyperactive state. Oftentimes, imbalances in our physical systems can make us more prone to fear, anxiety, and even unwanted psychic experiences. In such cases, Cayce recommended a treatment that emphasized physical intervention, such as massage and chiropractic adjustment. Even though there was no psychological event behind the fear, Cayce nevertheless recommended using affirmations and other forms of positive suggestion to reprogram the mind. For example, while receiving massage, the person might also visualize burdens dissolving and loving light replacing areas of stiff darkness. Whether or not there is anything to be afraid of or whether the fear is arising from a physical disturbance, there is the fact that the body is full of fear chemistry. Relaxation, however induced, is the prescribed remedy. Especially important, the mind needs to be fully participating in any physical treatment.

Sometimes an individual's diet can contribute to a physical source of fear. For example, Michael had been a regular coffee drinker all his life, with no negative effects. In his late forties, however, he began to notice an uncomfortable perspiration after his morning cups of coffee. He also noticed that his attitude toward the day ahead seemed to be more apprehensive than it used to be. Michael made the connection between the coffee, the perspiration, his attitude, and an overactive adrenal gland. He concluded that waking up by coffee was over-stimulating him. He changed his routine of several years and shifted his afternoon pleasure walk to a morning get up and wakeup walk. After returning from his walk, he would shower and meditate. Then he would drink his coffee and start his day. He found that with the new routine, there was no longer any negative effect from the coffee and that his usual upbeat approach to the day had returned.

Oftentimes, when individuals came to Mr. Cayce looking for help with their anxieties or fears, he would recommend inspirational reading. To be sure, there are all types of inspirational materials—everything from positive "thoughts for the day" to mainstays like *Daily Word* and scriptures from every religion. The scripture most often recommended by Edgar Cayce was the following: John, chapters 14, 15, 16 and 17; Psalms, chapters 1, 23, 24, 91; Exodus, chapter 19; and Deuteronomy, chapter 30.

The Cayce information is adamant that our dreams contain a wealth of information and guidance. In part, dreams contrast and correlate the events of the day, oftentimes giving the mind another perspective on events and experiences. In addition, dreams can give us guidance as to what we might do about a particular situation. Dreaming—itself—can be a healing experience. For example, most individuals have had the experience of going to sleep anxious, frustrated, or worried about something, only to awaken refreshed and revitalized; somehow the process of dreaming and sleeping has given the mind resolution. Just think how much more helpful that resolution might be if an individual was aware of what he or she had been dreaming. Recent research in "lucid dreaming" (the dream is considered lucid if the dreamer is aware and mindful that she or he is dreaming during the dream) has demonstrated that knowing "it is only a dream" allows some dreamers to actively combat and defeat their "demons" in a dream.

The readings often encouraged individuals to work with "presleep suggestion" for overcoming fears—especially as a helpful approach when working with children. For example, if your child suffers from night terrors, you might sit next to that child as he or she is falling asleep and be a voice of positive encouragement: "You are in a place of safety." "You will have a restful, helpful sleep." "You are home, and you are safe." And so forth. Presleep suggestion can be catered to address whatever is troubling an individual by replacing that with positive, reinforcing thoughts and ideas. Giving oneself suggestions when falling asleep is also a very effective strategy. We might decide to provide this kind of support to ourselves by using a recorder. It is most effective to record our own voice speaking the suggestions, as our subconscious will process it as us talking to ourselves.

Hypnosis, which provides a channel of communication between the conscious and subconscious mind, was a common prescription from Cayce for uncovering and reprogramming repressed fears. The channel of communication works in both directions. We can uncover information and also plant new ideas and motivations. Cayce suggested both strategies when dealing with fears.

In a demonstration using hypnosis to show how repressed fears operate, a hypnotist suggested to a hypnotized person that an apple they were holding was a live grenade about to explode if it was moved. The hypnotist gave the post-hypnotic suggestion that the person would not remember what happened while in hypnosis until the hypnotist sneezed. After the sneeze, the hypnotist suggested, the person would remember the session and no longer fear the apple. After the person came out of hypnosis, he looked around a bit, woke up, noticed the apple and had a panic reaction. Wanting to toss off the "grenade," but afraid of moving it, the person was paralyzed with fear. When the hypnotist sneezed, the person responds on cue, and looked at the apple and laughed.

Many folks who came to Cayce concerning their irrational fears were diagnosed as having repressed fears from childhood or past lives. Fred found himself, for example, very nervous and fearful for no reason around a new co-worker. Following the suggestions in the Cayce material, Fred sought out a psychologist who used hypnosis to uncover the source of the fear. While hypnotized, Fred described the co-worker as having a slight tic in the left eye. That observation immediately brought up a memory of a baby sitter Fred had as a young infant. The sitter, who had an eye tic, had been mean to him. That one session relieved the fear.

As to uncovering the source of repressed fears, hypnosis is not the only means available. Cayce noted that by simply asking ourselves, "I wonder where this fear came from?" we may find ourselves spontaneously remembering an incident from childhood. Meditation can also refine the process of remembering. Keeping steady with such an intention might even inspire a dream. Cayce noted that dreams can serve both functions—not only revealing the presence and source of an otherwise unrecognized fear, but also providing dream experiences that reduce or eliminate the fear.

When a thirty-five-year-old marine asked Edgar Cayce how to deal with his longstanding fears, Cayce recommended that he develop his sense of humor and attempt to see the "funny side" in life. Others were encouraged to laugh when they were depressed or discouraged, to read the funny papers, or to watch a funny movie. Oftentimes, laughter can provide immediate relief to tension.

Today, psychologists know that the basic challenge that fears present is that they keep the person away from situations where they would discover there was nothing to fear. The road from avoiding one's fear to facing and letting it go can take many paths. The most common is a combination of interventions that seek gradually two things simultaneously: to reduce fear and to bring the person a little closer to the object of fear. Dealing with nightmares is a good example of Cayce's approach, which is also supported by modern psychotherapeutic methods.

Suppose your child awakens from a nightmare of being chased by a lion. You put your child on your lap and comfort her or him, thus reducing the level of fear. Next you remind the child that you are present and nothing can hurt the child while you are around, thus providing a comforting affirmation. Then you ask the child to holler to the lion, "Leave me alone!" encouraging the child to use the protection of the parent as extra courage to confront the lion. A similar approach is used today for the treatment of post-traumatic shock among returning war veterans. The effect of the trauma shows itself in recurring nightmares. The therapy occurs in a group setting, where not only the therapist but the other veterans can support and encourage the patient to explore alternative ways of confronting the bogey appearing in the nightmare.

The dramatic example of treating nightmares encompasses all the main ingredients in Edgar Cayce's philosophy of dealing with fears in less dramatic situations. The first thing is to recognize and dedicate the fear to growing into closer alignment with spiritual truth and your co-creatorship with God. There are physical, mental, and spiritual means of temporarily lowering the fear level. As we use these methods, we must also use affirmations and guidance to move closer, little step by little step, to the rewards of overcoming the fear, to the enjoyment of being in harmony with the opportunities and events of life and able to respond and contribute as the creative individuals that by God's nature we are.

Cayce contended that everything happens for a purpose. With that in mind, adopting an "attitude of gratitude" toward adversities is also a good strategy for recovery and beyond. How might that same strategy apply to fear? To be aware that fear is present is the first step. Mindfulness of fear can be the first step in transforming it. Awareness of fear can be a wake-up call that we've fallen into the illusion of separation and all strategies for survival are probably tainted with fallacy. It can be a call for re-examination and re-dedication to our growth in co-creatorship with God. The fears that truly challenge us are those that come to our attention because they upset us, blocking us from doing something that we need or want to do. The person finds themselves in conflict, where the motivation to approach a situation is at war with a physically felt need to flee the situation.

In order to deal with our personal fears, Cayce provided many strategies. Regardless of the origin of the fear, these strategies were all designed to provide the individual with a means of taking charge of the situation, utilizing the power of the mind, setting aside the fear and replacing it with something more positive, and cultivating a new focus in the present. With this in mind, a new twist to Franklin Roosevelt's famous statement might simply be, "As I set aside my fear, I have nothing else to fear."

14

Cayce's Paradigm of Healing

Of the more than 14,000 readings on file in the Edgar Cayce archives, almost 9,000 deal with the topic of health and healing. Although known for his focus on holism and incorporating the entire individual (body, mind, emotions, and spirit) in the healing process, Cayce drew from every school of medicine. The Edgar Cayce Hospital for Research and Enlightenment (1928-1931) employed physicians, physiotherapists, body workers, nurses, and dieticians, and the readings themselves recommended every imaginable treatment: surgery, diet, massage, exercise, pharmacological, mindfulness, vibrational therapies, energy medicine, meditation, prayer, and much more. Cayce's formula for creation, "spirit is the life, mind is the builder, the physical is the result," is also his formula for health and healing. When we get sick, it is because conditions in the body have arisen that prevent the life force from flowing freely. These conditions must be addressed not just physically, but also mentally and spiritually.

In time, Dr. Harold J. Reilly, one of Cayce's contemporaries and a strong proponent of the health information in the readings, coined the acronym C.A.R.E. to describe the readings approach to preventative medicine and the underlying importance of involving each individual in her or his own healing process. Those initials stand for Circulation, Assimilation, Relaxation, and Elimination; and their overall importance is the establishment of health and the maintaining of personal wellness. However, even beyond the wide scope of information covered by the readings, the suggested treatment protocols, the insights that were literally decades ahead of their time, and the myriad of things each and every one of us can do to maintain personal wellness, there are deep principles at work that seem to come together to create Cayce's paradigm of healing.

Edgar Cayce's own psychic work began as he learned how to heal himself of a throat and voice problem through self-hypnosis. It should be no surprise, then, that his approach to healing is one that he shares with the story of hypnosis. It is a common, almost archetypal vision of health as being the result of the "life force" flowing through us. As perhaps a synonym for God or nature, the life force is health and vitality itself.

Hypnotism got its start as a search for the *Élan vital*—the vital life force—and a desire to harness it for healing. Early explorers of what became called "animal magnetism" were somewhat like modern day "tree huggers" who attempt to tap into the life force flowing through the tree's magnificent trunk. In Cayce's time, hypnosis had been streamlined to the use of suggestion. Some doctors had also employed "medical clairvoyants" to help them diagnose patients. Through the means of hypnosis, it was clear that the mind could communicate with the body and participate in healing. In Edgar Cayce's case, it was not considered surprising that Mr. Cayce, while in the hypnotic state, could summon forces within the body to bring an increased blood flow to his throat and heal his voice. Over time, his readings provided a great deal of information on healing, including the important role played by the patient in the healing process and the need to address the spiritual, mental, and physical components of the individual. In terms of unique concepts, he pointed out the role of the endocrine system as the bridge between emotions and bodily functioning. Thus he provided a handle on what would become a scientific revolution in medicine. Such revelations earned him the title, "father of holistic medicine."

We can get an insight into Cayce's overall approach to healing by considering a story that took place in 1972, at a historical meeting of many people concerned with new findings on consciousness and its role in the healing process. The place was Council Grove, Kansas, a spot that got its name from the practice of Native Americans to gather there for important meetings. The meeting was sponsored by the Menninger Foundation, a well-respected agency devoted to research on healing. In attendance at that meeting was a Native American named Rolling Thunder. He was there to share with others, for the first time, the Native American view on healing. As it turned out, he was also able to demonstrate it. One of the participants' sons had an accident on the grounds, seriously hurting his knee. Rolling Thunder agreed to perform a healing on the knee while everyone watched.

Rolling Thunder kneeled down to be at the boy's level and asked him about his knee. The boy explained how it happened and how it hurt. Rolling Thunder asked the boy why he wanted to have his knee healed. The boy answered that he wanted to be able to play soccer again. Rolling Thunder acknowledged that the boy had good reason to want to get well. He then began to treat the boy's knee with prayers and wrapping it with a beef steak. Afterwards he suggested that the boy go rest for a while before returning to his soccer game. A little while later in the conference, the boy was once again playing as before his injury.

After the demonstration, William McGarey MD, who at the time was co-director of the A.R.E. Clinic in Phoenix, addressed the audience. He was interested in the way Rolling Thunder spoke to the boy. In particular, he pointed out how Rolling Thunder asked the boy *why* he wanted to get well. Dr. McGarey stated that the same question had been posed by Edgar Cayce on a number of occasions and was a wonderful and straightforward example of what Edgar Cayce meant by addressing the spiritual in healing. It is not simply a matter of praying for healing; rather it is important for us to summon our purpose for healing, which naturally arouses our attention toward our purpose for living. Evoking purpose in that way places the healing in a much larger context than simply the physical problem.

As in every adversity or challenge, attempting to grasp the positive in the situation or seeing if it is possible to find a gift in illness can be a wonderful way to begin the healing process. As we might recall from Jesus' encounter with the blind man (John 9), illness offers us the opportunity to affirm our creative partnership with God as we assume the responsibility ourselves for being the conductor and facilitator of our own healing. Many of Cayce's suggestions for our role in healing mirror universal themes in humanity's search for meaning. Why are there illnesses and a need for healing? It is one way that the Creative Forces, through the activities of the Akasha and our response to these influences, teaches us that we've veered off the path and need to pay attention to the task of making a correction. In some way, we've gotten out of balance in our lives, and our body's functioning is trying to communicate that issue.

In the myths of the search for the Holy Grail—the cup that Jesus drank from at the Last Supper—there is a lesson about healing. In the stories, the king is not well, and thus the kingdom as a whole is suffering. All sorts of remedies are attempted, but nothing works. It takes the innocence of a fool, Parsifal, to ask the question of the king that no one had asked, "What ails you?" At the contemplation of that question, as the stories go, the king was healed and then subsequently died. Understood symbolically, the king stands for the governing ideal. It was no longer adequate to the task. For healing to occur, the first step is the honest acknowledgment that something is wrong, that you don't feel right—what is it? Turning one's attention inward in a sincere attitude of seeking is the beginning of healing. That the king died as he was healed suggests that healing required replacing the old ideal with a new one. With this in mind, one of the first principles at work in Cayce's paradigm of healing begins with awareness.

A second important principle is that there needs to be self-forgiveness. Cayce reminded us that Jesus spoke of healing through the forgiveness of sin. In this perspective, a sin is simply a mistake that produces consequences that operate as our teacher to help us move out of error and into truth. The transformation often requires accepting aspects of ourselves that previously had been unconscious thus bringing about a greater wholeness, which is the key ideal of healing.

A good example of this very principle comes from the revolutionary work of Carl Rogers. He began his career as a minister but shifted to counseling psychology. He believed that the important factors that allow spiritual faith to be a powerful influence in life came not from a church pulpit but from within a person. In order to demonstrate this belief, Rogers turned psychotherapy on its head by no longer offering advice and consultation to his clients. Instead, he "merely listened" to them, and watched as they unraveled their problems and found a healing source from within. His mode of listening was crucial. He found that most problems come about when a person's self-judgment begins to distort which aspects of a person gets to live and which do not. Such judgment, and the suppression or repression it brings about, has a person limping, in effect. As the person discusses his or her feelings, Rogers found that by his active listening, by reflecting back to the person what that person is expressing, but with an accepting tone and devoid of the judgment in the person's own voice, individuals came to be more accepting of their feelings. As self-acceptance allowed the person to experience and process more of their previously unaccepted feelings, they came into possession of a more complete set of data about themselves. As a result, they became more emotionally intelligent and were able to allow the life force full access for healing.

A third principle in the Cayce readings on healing is that we have a role in the healing process itself. Once we have become aware that something is ailing us, and then once we have let down our judgments and are honestly open with ourselves so that we can become better aware of guidance from within, we can begin a process of review.

Obviously, we are all responsible for such practical measures as diet and exercise, as well as working with attitudes, emotions, our own spiritual beliefs, and following through on recommended treatments; but in addition to that, modern research has confirmed that simply "getting it off your chest" can be very therapeutic. For example, the use of personal journaling to write out one's feelings about a given trauma can reduce the negative effects of that trauma. Research has shown that when given a chance to do journal writing about a past trauma, those whose writings addressed the trauma end up seeing a doctor significantly less often than those who avoided discussing the trauma in their journal writing. In that vein, Cayce also honors the fact that "humor is the best medicine." Using the principle of contrary conditioning, pairing the focus on trauma with the experience of humor and laughter can itself be healing. Making jokes about our own past trauma and its effects, when the time is right, can be very healing.

Our belief systems also play an important role. What we have faith in and believe can help heal us has a substantial impact upon healing itself. Cayce suggested that whatever belief one maintained regarding healing needed to be taken into account. For example, if you have a belief in one remedy versus another, or one physician versus another, or what will and won't work—all of these factors have an impact upon the healing process. Modern research has confirmed many of these same ideas in its use of placebos that demonstrate when someone possesses faith that something will work, the outcome is just as significant as actual medicine.

The fourth principle that Cayce would recommend is the importance of utilizing what he called the "imaginative forces" in any healing remedy. The mind plays an important role in our healing. Under the right conditions, we can communicate with our body through the subconscious mind to support the body's healing process. We may do so via meditation, hypnosis, visualization, or other forms of suggestion.

Along these lines, we can "raise the vibrations" of the body, to make it more amenable to change and healing. Edgar Cayce's work on the nature of vibratory energy has led to the field of "energy medicine," and the role of unseen forces in bringing about healing in the physical. Cayce noted that of all the things we could do physically to our bodies, we can best raise our physical vibrations by chanting—producing sensations of vibrations in our body through the use of our voice—especially when mentally holding the feeling of an ideal. As we hold that felt image of an ideal, and we allow that feeling to be expressed in a vibrato voice, not only does the physical body join in an attunement you can feel, the vibratory forces in the atoms of the body also become attuned. We'll discuss chanting in more detail later on.

We can also add visualization as another tool to personal healing. Using imagery as a means of affirming an ideal for healing, for affirming a normalization and harmonization in the body parts, is an important dimension to the healing process. At one time, science believed that we had control only over the "voluntary" nervous system. Today we realize that if given feedback, we can achieve control over a single nerve in the body. That kind of precise feedback needed to gain that level of control is not available to us except under special laboratory conditions. Yet with sufficient meditation, we can learn to be sensitive to shifts in how our body feels when we shift our perspective or attitude.

Using a simple example, when working on a construction project, we might hit our thumb with a hammer. Rather than cussing and continuing to work, we can use this opportunity to stop for a moment, taking time out to focus on our thumb, reaffirming its value to us in our work. We can sit back and relax for a while, staying mentally connected to our thumb as we allow the pain to subside. We may give thanks for the opportunity to reassess how we were approaching our work. Were we in too much of a hurry? During this time out, we can reconnect with our ideal and bring a feeling of it into our work, focusing on the pleasure of working the craft rather than the ego ideal of finishing quickly. Our wounded thumb then becomes a teacher for us, and we are better for it.

To understand ourselves to be somehow better for having experienced any health issue is the true measure and criterion for healing. When our intent is merely to undo the adversity, to get rid of the headache so we can continue as before, then the aspirin is merely a cure, a palliative treatment. When the aspirin is combined with time out and a brief meditation, it becomes an aid to a transformation in attitude. Work is taken up again but with a new mental set. That is healing. That is using the opportunity to reaffirm, re-experience, and reapply our co-creative relationship with God. Cayce's paradigm of healing includes a number of factors that call upon our joint participation in the healing process. In addition to understanding the patient's role in the healing process, the readings were decades ahead of their time in understanding the nature of illness and the workings of the human body.

15

Vibrations and Soul Expression

WE HEAR A LOT ABOUT "ENERGY" AND "VIBES" AND HOW CERTAIN people radiate good vibrations while others emit bad energy. Sometimes we use expressions like "that individual is a psychic drain," or "I feel really good just being around that person," or "he has great vibes." At some level, we understand that there is a correspondence between who an individual is and the kinds of energy or vibrations that she or he puts off. In fact, the Cayce information suggests that there is an interconnection between a person's soul and her or his personal vibrational pattern—a vibration that is as unique as a fingerprint.

We can imagine how vibrations might appear like the ripples on the surface of a lake when a stone is tossed into the water. Similarly, we can visualize how the vibrations of a tuning fork would appear as it oscillates in someone's hand. It is more difficult to imagine how the vibrations of people appear, but most individuals have a sense of the vibrations of certain people and even how those vibrations affect them. For example, imagine what kind of "vibes" we would pick up on while having lunch with a spiritual figure such as Gandhi or Mother Teresa, and how that experience would differ from being around a professional comedian or a politician running for re-election. The thoughts and activities of people create a vibration. Vibrations are a physical activity with an energetic effect that we can experience. At the same time, they also contain information that our sensory systems can perceive.

Scientists have confirmed with instrumentation that people pick up other people's moods in less than one second. They call it "emotional contagion." They theorize that it occurs through a process of unconscious mimicry, a natural empathic act that Cayce would call "attunement." When a person speaks, their voice projects vibrations. If another person intentionally attunes to the vibrations in the speaker's voice, the empathic listener will become aware of internal impressions, images, memories, and thoughts. In published research conducted with students of the Cayce material, the intuitive listener's impressions often contained information about the speaker's personality, life situation, and even past lives. Just as an individual can intentionally make an attunement, the listener can also cease the attunement and be free of any residual effects.

Of course not all vibrations are as obvious as the voice. Even when we are sitting next to someone silently, with our eyes closed, we still experience the vibrations at various levels. The same thing happens at a distance, as many scientific studies of psychic communication have confirmed. The Cayce information repeatedly noted that at the level of our subconscious minds, all humans are connected in the sense that what occurs in the subconscious of one person can affect the subconscious of anyone else. These effects are usually subliminal but we can bring them into awareness. Notice a sudden mood shift that seems without basis. By tuning into our imagination, we can experience images, memories, and other content that will reveal to us some of the information in that mood, and often its source is another person. By observing the mood in this way, we free ourselves from the subliminal contagion of the vibrations and turn it into something to examine for greater awareness.

There's a perfect example from scripture of how a person's faith can heal them combined with a demonstration of how vibration can affect someone. In Mark 5:24–34 is the story of a woman who suffered for twelve years with a physical ailment, spending a lot of her time and resources trying to get well. She had heard about the teachings of Jesus and, as a last resort, she decided to find him. She thought if she could simply touch the hem of his robe she would be healed, and when she did so, that's exactly what happened. How was that possible? The garment Jesus wore had picked up His vibrations, and because of the woman's faith, when she touched his robe, the healing energy passed into her.

It's important to realize that it's not just the garment of someone like Jesus that picks up energy. It's every piece of clothing we wear; it's all of our surroundings; it's every strand of hair upon our heads; it's every cell in our body. And these vibrations originate not only from our current attitudes and emotions but also from the history of the soul's experiences. Research in several laboratories has confirmed that it is possible to "imprint" material with thoughts or intentions so that the material shows a physical effect of such imprinting. Blessing water with healing intent, for example, changes the crystalline structure of the water. While scientific theory explaining the process lags behind, evidence accumulates concerning its reality. It is common to hear of "quantum" theories, as scientists attempt to understand the role of consciousness in the relationship between energy and matter.

The Edgar Cayce material offers a perspective on this question—that mental patterns precipitate energy into material forms. When energy combines with patterns of thought, some new unique form of creation takes place. No matter how this process will be ultimately understood, it is clear that material objects have a "memory" of the information contained in vibrational influences.

Cayce told one woman who was having problems with hypertension and arteriosclerosis that the vibration of those illnesses had essentially become a part of her surroundings to such an extent that if she moved out of her home, whoever next lived in her house would be susceptible to those very same illnesses. The vibration would remain as a sort of residue. Another woman, who really liked to wear jewelry when she went out, had come to Edgar Cayce for help with severe depression. He told her that the reason she kept having relapses was because whenever she was feeling better she put on her jewelry—jewelry that had been imprinted with the vibration of depression—and that her own jewelry was ultimately re-infecting her.

The good news in this situation is that it is possible to cleanse the undesirable vibrations unintentionally imprinted into an object. To do so, a person needs to intentionally imprint positive, healing, and cleansing information into the object. Ritual acts that are meaningful to the person and which intensify the reality of the imprinting process—such as meditation, uplifting music, prayer, energy work, and washing the object—can all help.

In addition to the vibrations of individuals, the collective vibrations of people eventually imprint buildings, locations, and even cities and countries. For example, the energetic feeling inside a church, a synagogue, a temple, or a mosque—even when empty—is very different from the energy and vibrations inside a post office or a shopping mall. Cayce contended that the very thoughts of individuals possess a vibration, ultimately leading to the creation of "crimes or miracles" because of the energy put off by those very thoughts and intentions. Thus we have the reality that Cayce refers to repeatedly: "Thoughts are things." Therefore, in his discourses on spiritual growth, he emphasizes the importance of cultivating our thoughts in a constructive manner.

For spiritual and personal growth, Cayce prescribed daily working with spiritual ideals, working with personal attunement, and working with personal application. One byproduct of personal and spiritual growth, from the readings' perspective, is an improvement in vibrations.

Perhaps the greatest contribution that the Cayce information gave to the topics of soul growth and the raising of personal vibrations was the creation of the *A Search for God* Study Group program. The background of this life-transformative, ecumenical program can be traced back to September 1931, when a group of ordinary people met with Edgar Cayce in an effort to learn how each of them could work personally with insights and information contained in the Cayce readings. None of the group members could have possibly imagined the impact that meeting and their subsequent gatherings—nearly fifty meetings for the first twelve lessons—would have upon the rest of their lives, nor could the group have foreseen the effect of their work upon the lives of hundreds of thousands of others even decades later.

Study Group #1—as they called themselves—worked for years to compile twelve essays in spirituality. The first lesson was "Cooperation," and the others were assembled in sequential order before finally being published in 1942 as *A Search for God, Book I.* The group's intent was to work with the material so it could be applied, understood, even "lived" in their daily lives. It was their hope that universal concepts might somehow be practically applied in such a manner as to bring a true awareness of the living Spirit into everyday life. The end result has been that these lessons in spirituality have been called one of the earliest and most effective tools for personal transformation introduced into the Western Hemisphere. These lessons in spirituality emphasize the oneness of all life, a love and tolerance for all people, as well as a compassion and understanding for every major religion of the world.

What is perhaps most valuable about the Study Group material is that it is essentially a manual for individual growth and development and for raising consciousness and personal vibration. In total, there are twenty-four lessons (the second set of twelve lessons, contained in book II, have been called a higher vibration of the first twelve lessons). Today, many decades after the first Study Group began, there are a variety of ways to participate (go to EdgarCayce.org for more information on Study Groups).

Edgar Cayce suggested that there are essentially three primary tools for spiritual growth: ideals, attunement, and application. As was mentioned earlier, he also recommended chanting, especially for personal attunement. In fact, Cayce suggested that by using our voice, we can improve our vibrations more than by any other physical means. Two chants frequently recommended in the readings for attunement and raising personal vibrations are "Arrr-Reeee-Ohmmmm," as well as just simply "Ohmmmmmmm."

Cayce recommended using simple vowel sounds to learn how our voice can be used to affect the vibrations in our body–mind. By chanting, we use our voice to provide a medium for the vibrations to become even more physically active within us. We often use the phrases, "raising vibrations" and moving to "higher consciousness." Cayce had the opportunity to explain to us that these metaphors, "raising" and "higher," are not to be taken literally. These optimal vibrations are intertwined with the soul–self and lie dormant within us, he explained, waiting to be activated by our attuning to our ideals. Although the image of being "raised higher" draws its meaning from experiences at higher altitudes, such as mountaintops, where we might gain a more peaceful and wider perspective on things, these metaphors are intended to invoke in us thoughts and feelings concerning our ideals. We could focus on the ideal of love, for example, and as we feel this consciousness developing in our awareness, we can give voice to the feeling by toning aloud a vowel sound (using your voice to make drawn-out sounds for healing), such as "Ahh" or "Ohh." As we allow our voice to express the feeling in our ideal, the vibrations in our voice then begin to imprint our body-mind with the pattern of that ideal. We grow in bodily consciousness of that ideal and it becomes more real. Our first act of expressing the ideal in physicality, through the voice, aids in our attunement to that ideal and its expression in other activities.

In regard to using the soul-growth material for improving personal vibrations, begin by imagining a type of person helpful to emulate in life—a more loving person with more understanding, more patience, a better listener. . . whatever it might be. Imagine someone who best embodies your spiritual ideal right now. Imagine how it must feel to be this person. Contemplate and experience the attitudes and thoughts this person would hold in mind, as well as the activities he or she would exemplify in relationships with others. Attitudes and activities bring spiritual ideals into living manifestation. As we use our imagination to create an idealized role model, it is important to feel the energy of this ideal in our body. Doing so, the vibrations associated with that ideal begin to imprint themselves upon us. You can also encourage these vibrations into having a greater impact by chanting. There develops a synergistic effect, for the more you feel the ideal within, the more the voice expresses that ideal in its vibrations, and the more those vibrations are imprinted upon the body-mind, leading to the greater possibility of living the ideal.

If I decided, for example, that I wanted to pick a spiritual ideal that embodied becoming more compassionate, I might imagine the most compassionate person I have ever met. I would imagine how that person might feel, or what it might feel like to be around such a person. As I imagine the vibrations, I use my voice to give sound to that vibration. As I chant, feeling the vibrations growing within me, I ask some questions. What kinds of thoughts do I think that compassionate person held in mind? What might this compassionate person think of this challenging situation I am dealing with right now? And how might a compassionate person respond to a particular person or problem? What would a compassionate person say to a challenging individual at work? What affirmations or meditation verses would a compassionate person focus upon? And so forth.

As I imagine how an individual who embodies the spiritual ideal I hope to manifest would respond to life in various situations, and impress upon myself the vibrations that create and express such a pattern, I see myself propelled and guided by those vibrations to then act accordingly. At any time I can review this process, strengthen my familiarity with those vibrations, and in time I will become very much like the person I'm hoping to emulate. Perhaps the most important aspect of all this is to begin acting in application like the person I hope to become. Thus I can ride the vibrations to a more spiritual quality of consciousness and express my soul's ideals through my personal growth.

The Cayce information suggests that ultimately we heal or harm each individual with whom we come in contact by the vibration we emit. Ultimately, our vibration has that same type of impact upon the world at large. At any point in time, our vibration is essentially the sum total of everything that the soul has experienced, believed, applied, and thought. Our vibration changes through life's experiences and our own spiritual growth. The premise put forth in the readings is that one of the ultimate goals in life is to somehow give expression to the soul's individuality while we are in the earth—thereby bringing spirit into the earth. To this end, each individual has the capacity to manifest a unique vibration that somehow reflects the very image of the divine.

16

Jesus as a Pattern for Humankind

A CENTRAL PREMISE IN THE EDGAR CAYCE MATERIAL IS THAT THE LIFE
of Jesus has relevance for all individuals, regardless of their religious
beliefs or backgrounds. What may be surprising, however, is that this
relevance is not about religion; instead, it is about the ultimate nature
of humankind and our collective destiny as children of God. The readings suggest that an overarching purpose for incarnating in the earth
is to acquire and perfectly manifest an awareness of the soul's oneness
with God. This is the purpose that Jesus fulfilled, becoming an example
for each and every soul. For this reason, the readings suggest each of us
may need to reexamine the life and mission of Jesus afresh.

Perhaps the greatest challenge in taking another look at the life
of Jesus is that most of us, whether Christian or non-Christian, have
preconceived notions about this individual that may be difficult to
overcome. In part, it is a matter of definitions—the words "Jesus" and
"Christ" have acquired meanings from both history and personal experience that may not necessarily agree with definitions put forth by
the readings. Over the years, these terms have also been misused, and
certainly individuals have done horrendous things in the name of

Jesus that are completely contrary to the premise of manifesting a full awareness of spirit in the earth. Rather than defining Jesus in terms of religion, however, Cayce states instead that Jesus was a man who manifested the Christ Consciousness: "the awareness within each soul, imprinted in pattern on the mind, and waiting to be awakened by the will, of the soul's oneness with God." (5749-14) Depending upon our personal associations, we might decide to call this "God Consciousness" to describe the same thing. For example, in Vedanta Hinduism it could be labeled as the Atman or the true individual self. Ultimately, whatever the term, the consciousness is about becoming aligned with the divine and returning to a state of wholeness.

This same concept that we are all in the process of returning to a state of wholeness and atonement with the divine is told in a variety of archetypal stories and tales, including the Parable of the Prodigal Son (Luke 15:11-24). Simply stated, the parable describes how we were with God in the beginning. Through the power of our free will, we made choices that were not necessarily in perfect accord with the Creator. However, these choices were essentially a learning experience or journey—one that enables us to grow and awaken to our true heritage. At some point, each of us will "arise" and decide to return to God, regaining our inheritance, and finally experience our rightful relationship with Him.

From a psychological perspective, this process in consciousness growth might be described as personal development or self-realization. Carl Jung (1875-1961), founder of the analytical school of psychology, called the Christ "the archetype of the self" for the Christ-figure exemplified the self fully realized: "He represents a totality of a divine or heavenly kind, a glorified man, a son of God . . . unspotted by sin." [Carl Jung. *Aion: Researches into the Phenomenology of Self (Collected Works, Vol. 9, Part 2)*. Princeton University Press, 1979]. Rather than being a message restricted to a specific religion, the Christ instead embodies a universal archetype of the self for all of humankind. This is essentially the premise put forth by the Cayce readings that regardless of an individual's religious or personal beliefs, the Christ pattern exists in potential upon the very fiber of our being. It is that unique portion of us that remains in perfect accord with the Creator and is simply waiting to find expression in the earth.

From this perspective, seeing Jesus as a pattern for humankind may be helpful in the same way that an older sibling can sometimes provide insight and counsel into life's difficulties because he or she went through them first. The readings present Jesus as the "elder brother" to all of humanity—a soul who came to show each one of us the way back to our spiritual Source by perfectly manifesting the laws of the Creator. Part of his mission was to demonstrate fully the living awareness of the spirit in the earth. As Cayce once told a group of individuals, "For all have the pattern, whether they call on that name or not."

Another issue that can be equally problematic regarding Jesus is the obvious question as to whether or not He was truly the Son of God. For centuries, Christians have emotionally affirmed yes, and non-Christians have just as emotionally responded no. But even among Christians, additional questions have often only complicated the issue as to just how different Jesus is from the rest of us: If He became (hu)man, doesn't that suggest He was like us? But if He was like us, how could He be God? Generally the answer has fallen somewhere in between: He was like us, and yet not like us. The Edgar Cayce readings offer another alternative: Not only was Jesus a son of God, but the relationship Jesus shared with the Creator is also true for each and every one of us. We are all God's children and ultimately one child is no different than any other. In other words: Jesus was like each one of us, and ultimately each one of us is destined to be like Him. Ironically, what this suggests is that for more than 2,000 years, much of humankind has been trying to make a man out of Jesus, when His whole goal was to show us the ultimate divinity within each and every one of us!

Before becoming offended by this incredible possibility, know that evidence for this premise is found not only in the Edgar Cayce material but also in the Bible. For example, when speaking about humankind, Jesus states, "They are not of the world, even as I am not of the world," (John 17:16). He also affirms that the claims He makes about himself and His connection to God are true for each and every soul: "That they all may be one; as thou, Father, art in me, and I in thee, that they also may be one in us: that the world may believe that thou hast sent me. And the glory which thou gavest me I have given them; that they may be one, even as we are one . . . " (John 17:21-22) We also read in John 10:30-34: "I and my Father are one. Then the Jews took up stones again to stone him. Jesus answered them, 'Many good works have I shewed you from my Father; for which of these do ye stone me?' The Jews answered him, saying, 'For a good work we stone thee not; but for blasphemy; and because that thou, being a man, makest thyself God.' Jesus answered them, 'Is it not written in your law, I said, Ye are gods.'" This reference is to the Old Testament, specifically the 82nd Psalm, which asserts that not only are we God's children, but we are also "gods" (to be sure in-the-making), as well. Although some religious individuals may be offended by the statement that everyone is a part of God, in recent years more and more individuals have found some truth in the premise that somehow everything in the universe is connected.

In the classic book *Cosmic Consciousness: A Study in the Evolution of the Human Mind*, Dr. Richard Maurice Bucke detailed numerous accounts of mystical experiences that seemed to suggest the existence of a divine consciousness that had been experienced by individuals throughout history. Dr. Bucke became convinced that cosmic consciousness had little to do with an individual's specific religious background and (writing in the third person) alluded to the impact his own personal experience would have upon the rest of his life:

> " . . . he saw and knew that the Cosmos is not dead matter but a living Presence, that the soul of man is immortal, that the universe is so built and ordered that without any peradventure all things work together for the good of each and all, that the foundation principle of the world is what we call love and that the happiness of every one is in the long run absolutely certain." [Richard Maurice Bucke. Cosmic Consciousness: A Study in the Evolution of the Human Mind. Dutton, 1959]

From a practical standpoint, what does Jesus as a pattern for humankind mean for each of us individually? The readings told Thomas Sugrue, author of the 1942 Edgar Cayce biography, *There Is a River*, that the pattern was best emulated by living in accord with the fruits of the spirit, such things as love, gentleness, kindness, patience, and long-suffering (i.e., determined endurance). On another occasion, when an individual wanted to expand Cayce's work with the readings to address specific illnesses and help large numbers of people rather than having to deal with one individual at a time, the readings stated unequivocally that Jesus' approach to service, one individual at a time, was the best approach: "He took them as they came, pretty good pattern to follow."

It is not simply a matter of making an effort to follow a pattern. It is also a matter of preparing yourself to allow the pattern itself to inform and guide your relationship to life. For what we are calling a pattern here is actually a living force—what we might call, in Edgar Cayce's perspective, the force of the Creator's intention that we become companions with the Creator; or as might be expressed by contemporary philosophers and scientists, the force of the evolutionary intent that is governing the growth of consciousness among human beings. In his inspired state of mind, Cayce anticipated the modern thinkers who are shaping our approach to the future.

Carl Jung, for example, through analysis of ancient religious texts, concluded that there is a God, and that this God is seen in His attempts to become conscious in human beings. Ken Wilber, a major transpersonal philosopher, postulated an evolutionary hierarchy in which life experiences itself in increasing degrees of self-consciousness. The stage after the current one is where humans experience the sum total of their individual consciousnesses in an integrated manner, reminiscent of how Cayce described the consciousness held by Jesus, "to know yourself to be yourself and yet one with God, even as Jesus." Theoretical physicists speculate about the role of consciousness in the evolution of the universe, noting that consciousness allows the universe to be observed, and thus creation becomes conscious of itself over time. These various perspectives have in common that there is a general, evolutionary tendency toward the very consciousness that Cayce describes as defining Jesus' state of mind. The implication is that if we set an ideal to grow in a manner consistent with the Jesus pattern, there is evolutionary force within that pattern that will help implement the intention.

What may be most revolutionary about Cayce's approach to Jesus is the idea that our individual "salvation" comes only from emulating the pattern of this soul and completely aligning with our oneness with God. The readings offer a revision of Jesus' life that provides a way for Christians to see the ultimate universal truth that is expressed in all religions, and at the same time allows non-Christians to see how Jesus reflects the universal truths that are contained in their own faiths. In fact, while discussing the variety of faiths available to humankind, Cayce asked "what is the difference?"—for all Truth inevitably comes from the same source. Ultimately, in any given incarnation, individuals are drawn to that faith which might best provide the learning environment the soul needs in its consciousness growth.

The Jesus we find in the Edgar Cayce readings is an elder brother, a way-shower, and a pattern for all of humankind. Ultimately, this Jesus is an example for each and every soul. The example is one of a growth in consciousness through living in accord with a pattern of the fully realized self. This pattern exemplifies the very best traits that we might associate with a compassionate, all-loving, understanding, forgiving, and nurturing human being. These traits somehow embody aspects of God or Christ Consciousness—a consciousness that is our collective destiny.

17

The Soul's Affinity for Co-Creation

ONE OF THE MOST INTERESTING AND AT THE SAME TIME GLOSSED over concepts contained in the Edgar Cayce readings deals with the soul's affinity for co-creation. Cayce's premise is that each of us is a co-creator with the Creator, God, and ultimately a companion with this Creator. Unfortunately, we may fail to fully understand the far-reaching implications of this capacity in our present experience, because it is only our knack for perpetual co-creation that will enable us to transform ourselves and, in turn, transform the world. And it is only as we embrace our co-creativity that we can become companions with the Creator.

When individuals first encounter the idea that we were created to be companions and co-creators with God, the possibility of such a destiny may certainly have an intellectual appeal. We are all daughters and sons of the divine! Over the years, many individuals have cited Edgar Cayce's admonition that each individual was ultimately created to become a companion and co-creator with the divine. However, we may have simply spoken the words rather than coming to a full realization of their meaning. Perhaps we have allowed ourselves to believe that this co-creative ability is something far off—something that will be ours when we reach "perfection." Some may claim that they don't really feel worthy of such a relationship. After all, there are a number of things about all of us that are not really "godlike." There are many temptations to deny or ignore our co-creativity.

Because of the challenges of the times in which we live, it is not surprising that so many of us may feel overwhelmed by life and our personal experiences. There appear to be challenges of every nature surrounding us—in society, in our communities, and in the world. A few headlines from any news source make the challenges of contemporary life abundantly clear. On a personal level, we may find ourselves overwhelmed by relationship problems, financial difficulties, job insecurities, family tragedies, and all manner of physical, mental, and spiritual challenges and even suffering. Perhaps it is because of these incredible personal challenges that one may adopt a helpless feeling that "there is nothing I can do about it." This victim consciousness can also come into play when we discuss the subject of karma. We may feel as if we (or others) have encountered a particular situation because of karma and that there is nothing that can be done to change it.

We may also find ourselves responding to life as a bystander rather than utilizing the soul's affinity for co-creation. Our bystander mentality comes to the forefront whenever we see a horrendous headline or a disaster being highlighted on the news and our response is simply to change the channel or turn the page. Because of the preponderance of this kind of information, we have perhaps become conditioned to accept the inevitability or even normalcy of all manner of crime and human tragedy.

This bystander approach entails the belief that we can do very little, if anything, to affect politics, the environment, issues of terrorism, the energy problem—whatever the concern may be, whether it is personal, local, or global. As a bystander, we may remain unaware of the people around us who could utilize our help—even if it is only to lend an ear. We disempower ourselves by choosing not to vote, believing we can't make a difference. We overlook our connection to all of humankind by simply turning on the TV to observe the direction of a storm, or to witness some horrendous tragedy on the news without taking the time to pray that the storm might be dissipated or that those who are suffering might somehow be comforted.

If our newspapers, TVs, and Internet news feeds are competing with fearful headlines to capture our attention, while ignoring less "newsworthy" stories about human kindness, what kinds of thoughts and ideas are becoming part of our overall perception? The Cayce readings are adamant in their stance that "thoughts are things and may become crimes or miracles!" Are our thoughts creating miracles for the future, or are we contributing to possible disaster?

Regardless of our conscious level of spiritual awareness, there is a co-creative spark within each and every individual that is part of one's personal birthright. It is always engaged and cannot be avoided. We are not referring merely to ways of being "creative," such as in the arts, cooking, gardening, relationships, or business. Our co-creativity is a basic aspect of our being a conscious part of the living physical planet, and it is something that we cannot escape. It is through our choices that we are constantly co-creating with God. Our use of free will introduces an unpredictable, creative element to the unchangeable laws of cause and effect. Each time we make a choice, we set in motion a chain of events, with both intended and unintended consequences.

Science has demonstrated that there is a determinism that governs the activity of physical life. The law of cause and effect holds for the actions of material objects. Yet there is also indeterminacy—an aspect of creation that is not governed by the law of cause and effect. These two aspects exist in God and also in us.

The Creator God has, as Edgar Cayce revealed, the impersonal aspect, which the readings portrayed as a Force. This impersonal aspect drives the physical facets of the universe, including our bodies and the effects of our actions. Then there is the personal dimension of God, which Cayce portrayed as the loving Parent. This dimension is usually equated with the "I Am" presence within. Individually, the "I Am" or "Silent Witness" within is experienced as an observer, the consciousness within that is aware. It is this awareness that monitors all that happens, both within us and around us. And it is this awareness that pertains to the indeterminate dimension of life.

Science has explored the interaction of these two dimensions in its observation of atoms and their behavior. Although science can predict much of an atom's behavior by looking at forces that touch upon it and cause that behavior, there are also times when the atom's behavior cannot be predicted. Instead, scientists have discovered that it is not until they actually observe the atom that the atom "decides" what to do. Before the observation, the atom is in an "indeterminate" state of being. We have a similar characteristic. Many of our choices cannot be predicted, they remain indeterminate. Our God-given free will is the basis of this indeterminacy. God does not know our choices, but once we make a choice, the laws of the universe determine the effect of our actions. Our very choice, then, is a creative act, an action that collaborates with the laws of the universe to bring about a determined effect. It is our free will—our power of choice—that binds us to the co-creative role. The question is not, then, Will we be co-creators? The question is, What kind of co-creation will we produce?

What is important to understand is that the soul's birthright of co-creative expression is not something relegated to the afterlife or a byproduct of soul perfection. In actuality, whether or not we fully appreciate it, both individually and collectively, we already are co-creative; but we have not yet become aware of, and acted appropriately with, this potential. With this in mind, as a co-creator, how are we responding to life in the here and now? And perhaps more importantly, as co-creators, what are we building for our tomorrows?

It is not what happens to us that has the strongest impact upon our lives but instead how we choose to respond to what happens to us. Regardless of our present situation or difficulties, the readings affirm that because of the soul's creative capacity, we are always co-creating the future, and there is always the possibility of hope and change.

Cayce's approach to our co-creative abilities is one that constantly builds for the future. Regardless of our present circumstance, regardless of current world events, regardless of how overwhelmed we may feel right now, the readings contend that there is something we can do about it. The simplest approach to conscious and intentional co-creation that comes out of the Cayce readings is: Do what you know to do, and the next step will be given. As a means of addressing the environment, in practical terms this might simply mean choosing paper bags over plastic bags at the grocery store—or better yet, bringing our own. Maybe we can pick up trash when we see it on the ground. In terms of energy conservation, we might decide to stop driving to the shopping center every time we need something and instead wait until there are several items on our list; we may choose to turn our thermostats to more conservative settings. As it relates to health care, we could become more proactive in our own exercise, diet, and health routines. In terms of terrorism, at the very least, we might become more cognizant of the beliefs we may have in common—even with those who seem so different from us.

Edgar Cayce encouraged individuals to "make the world a better place" because they have lived in it. That's co-creation. Cayce also encouraged individuals to "pray and live as you pray" and to "give God a chance" in terms of helping to create their lives. When an individual once asked Edgar Cayce how to be of the greatest service to humankind, the response was simply to begin working with the daily practice of prayer and meditation. That's working with our capacity for co-creation!

As an example of working with co-creation, when Janet found herself in a predicament, caught between the competing demands of her job and her family, she felt overwhelmed and helpless. She was beginning to resent those she loved and felt guilty about her devotion to her career. She realized that she was harboring destructive emotions, but didn't know what to do about it. She recognized that feelings of powerlessness don't reflect the facts so much as they reflect an attitude. For days she meditated on her situation, and prayed for an approach that would meet the needs of her loved ones, support her career, and give her a needed sense of satisfaction with herself. Her meditations reminded her that she knew how to stay centered in her interactions with family members by focusing on being a good listener, and that they would appreciate this kind of attention. So she made "listening" her creative response to her predicament until she was shown her next step. One day, she realized that she was listening to her work supervisor in a new way. As a result she heard, for the first time, the real intent behind the supervisor's frequent comment to "take it easy." Janet realized that her supervisor was pleased with her work and was encouraging her to slow down a bit, and that she didn't need to take on as much as she had been doing. This revelation about her supervisor's attitude toward Janet's work was like a dust mop gathering up cobwebs in her mind, old assumptions about her worth and her need to always prove herself.

Not only was she coming into closer contact with a more authentic sense of self, but she found that she felt free of her "predicament," and instead felt proud of her ability to nurture both a family and a career, making a difference to many people, including herself.

Not only are we actively building our tomorrows, but we are collectively creating the future of the world and all of humankind. From a reincarnation worldview, we are also creating the world we will come back to. What do we want the world of the future to look like?

Right now, we can respond consciously to life as a co-creator. We can realize that we are every bit responsible for shaping the course of our lives. We can see everything about us as a reflection of what we need to work on as well as a testament to how we've been doing with this business of co-creation.

When someone asks questions like, "When do you think we will have peace on earth?" Or, "When do you think we will really have an Age of Enlightenment?" Tell them that there is only one answer: When we have helped to create it! The truth of the matter is that we are responsible for the present, which was once our future. What do we want the world of tomorrow to look like? What are we co-creating for our next future? Where do we want to go as a collective humanity?

Our future as co-creators is not something far off. Our future as co-creators is actively formed by our thoughts, our deeds, and our interactions today. Yes, we are at the dawn of a New World. But it will only be ours as we bring it to pass. As co-creators in the here and now, we need to become consciously aware of our role in its creation. We can accomplish anything, working together as conscious co-creators. When you consider our true nature, this really is not so amazing. We are divine children of a loving Creator. We are here to bring spirit into the earth. As long as we are incarnate, we have the possibility to effect lasting, positive change.

Today, we are facing perhaps the greatest challenge of our history in the earth, and that challenge isn't ultimately about earthquakes or global upheavals or crime or terrorism or political divisions or the economy or the environment. Ultimately, our greatest challenge is whether or not we can become consciously aware of the impact we have upon our present experience. What kind of a world are we building? Our collective future is within our hands. What are we doing about it?

18

Psychic Is of the Soul

THE EDGAR CAYCE MATERIAL FREQUENTLY DISCUSSES THE CORRELATION between personal soul growth and the manifestation of psychic abilities. That connection is evident in the readings on soul growth, it is part of his oft-quoted statement "psychic is of the soul," and it is inferred in a variety of ways in which empathy for others became the psychic conduit through which valid and helpful information was obtained for someone in need. Whereas it is perhaps logical when pursuing the topic of psychic functioning to put the focus on mental "techniques," such as that found in altered states of consciousness, Cayce's own motivation was always coming from his soul's desire to know companionship with the Creator directly and through his relationships with others. In spite of the fact that Cayce had countless personal psychic experiences in his own life, his goal was not to demonstrate the wonders of his psychic prowess but to instead provide a channel of assistance to those who came to him for help.

Harmon Bro, a psychologist and educator who worked with Edgar Cayce and had the opportunity to observe hundreds of readings, came to understand that Cayce was much more interested in "relationship" than he was in "power." A voracious letter writer, Cayce kept up a personal correspondence with many of the readings' recipients and encouraged them in their personal life's paths. His office was also filled with snapshots of scores of individuals who had sought his help.

Cayce's approach to the manifestation of psychic ability suggests a contrast that is today recognizable as the difference between a masculine–ego orientation (I am because of my autonomy) and a female–ego orientation (I am because of my relationships). Cayce's "psychic is of the soul" affirmation is both very idealistic and a forerunner of a postmodern perspective on the nature of the individual self. Simply stated, you might choose to go elsewhere to learn about psychic "tricks," but you can choose to follow Cayce's path of psychic functioning if your ultimate goal is to awaken your soul to its true relationship with other people and the Creator.

Ironically, it is because of this interconnectedness between relationship and psychic ability that the scientific study of ESP has often been difficult to validate. First of all, an attitude of curiosity such as "Let's see if I can do this…" creates an ego involvement in one's performance—an extreme distraction from what optimally stimulates psychic functioning. Entering any psychic experiment with the ultimate focus being on self's ability to perform the task is counterproductive. Secondly, most ESP experiments are devoid of the kind of motivation that facilitates intuition. Enticing the soul's involvement is about more than curiosity regarding the color of a card, for example, which could easily be determined by turning it over to look at it. If psychic ability is an attribute of the soul, as presented by Cayce, then the tool that can move psychic functioning to the forefront is relationships—our relationship and interconnection with self, with others, and with our Creator.

Demonstrating the importance of relationship and empathy in the psychic process, Cayce told one individual that if he truly wanted to experience the "key to telepathy," he needed to find a friend to work with for twenty days. At the same time each day, he and his friend were to sit quietly and think about one another. They were to imagine each other and to try to feel what that other individual had been doing just prior to the agreed upon time for the daily exercise. They were to do this every day for twenty days. At the end of that period, Cayce assured him that both he and his friend would have gained firsthand experience with understanding the psychic connection.

To be sure, Cayce described that we can, as soul beings, also derive information directly from the universal consciousness, just as he did. More often, however, the information was derived via the connection that exists between all subconscious minds. Our individual subconscious is aware of everything going on within the body. The subconscious also has access to soul memories. Cayce noted that he obtained information in two basic ways: One was to attune himself to the subconscious mind of another person. The second was his ability to read what has been called the Akashic Records, where everyone's thoughts and actions create marks or energetic signatures upon the skein of time and space.

Let's briefly consider some of Cayce's own psychic feats. He could diagnose his own medical condition and that of others, including describing neuropsychological processes that would not be discovered and understood by medical science until years later. He predicted the stock market crash and a number of changes in world affairs that we are experiencing today, including the rise of China as a global superpower. He described effective medical remedies that were unknown to medical science. He could provide information from an individual's past lives and explain how that past life experience was affecting the person in the present. He could describe ancient civilizations in great detail. He gave an account of the meaning and purpose of creation that anticipated the thinking of modern philosophers. He could describe the location of a lost object and the whereabouts of a missing person. He could not, however, always distinguish between a person's thoughts and actions without taking into account other information. Nor could he locate an oil well in order to further subsidize his own work. Although his "misses" appear to be few, they do suggest that psychic ability is not simply an all or nothing process.

When asked to describe how his psychic ability functioned, he noted these aspects: There is the ability to set self aside. There is the ability to make an attunement to the desired object of information. There is the capacity to receive impressions. There is the ability to organize or recognize the meaning of the impressions. A related ability is to bring to the conscious level those impressions, where the mind can translate those impressions into words and use language to describe them. The basic principle of Cayce's approach to intuition might be described, as follows: Spirituality has the force of the evolution of consciousness behind it. Psychic ability is but a tool of consciousness. Learning to develop this tool in service to others will prove helpful to the growth of your own spiritual awareness. Ultimately, your ideal should be to learn to know and be your true individual self and at the same time recognize your oneness with "All That Is." In trying to "train" or exercise your psychic sense, don't just be good, but be good for something. Rather than trying to "open yourself to psychic experiences," instead attempt experiments using psychic ability to achieve constructive goals. Learn to "watch self go by," as Cayce put it, to be passively mindful of the flow from the subconscious mind: meditation, prayer, and dream work are all very helpful. Balance serving self and others.

Another aspect of Cayce's formulation is the attunement process. Tuning in has two components: one being the person we are seeking information for (e.g., having an empathetic connection with that individual) and the second is obtaining the information that is being sought. Edgar Cayce's term for such attunement was that we should "become one with" the person. Ultimately, of course, the mission of the soul is to realize its oneness with God and all creation, so it should not come as a surprise that the ideal psychic exercises would involve the challenge of expanding what we can become one with. We find it is an act of the imagination, as we use our imagination to place ourselves "in the shoes" of the other person. To be sure, this process is an act of empathy, and thus is right on track with the soul's mission to improve its relations with others. Cayce provides a valid approach: "the purpose of the heart is to know yourself to be yourself and yet One with God." (281-37)

On more than a dozen occasions the readings also prescribed a means of acting upon the premise that "psychic is of the soul" for obtaining intuitive guidance for one's self. In part, the process seems very straightforward, but it is also a way for the individual to develop a closer relationship with self while gaining practical experience in attunement. Essentially, the approach can be used for any question in which the answer can be framed in terms of a "yes" or a "no." Cayce advised thinking about the situation and then using one's logic and mental abilities to simply decide "yes" or "no." After making a preliminary decision, the question was to be set aside. Sometimes, Cayce told the individual to put his or her mind on something else for a while; on other occasions, Cayce recommended moving right ahead to the second step. After making a conscious choice as to the best decision, the next step was for the individual to spend some quiet time in meditation and prayer—a personal time of attunement when the whole issue was to be set aside. After having time in meditation, your attuned self was to then repeat the question and ask, "Yes or no?" Edgar Cayce stated that this was a great way to work with intuition within one's self, and whenever you came to the same conclusion as your conscious decision then you could rest assured that the choice was correct. If the decisions were different, then the individual needed to revisit the entire issue and give it additional thought, meditation, and prayer.

Continuing the theme that the psychic process is best experienced through relationship, when Cayce was asked how to become psychic like he was, his response was to design a small group curriculum in spirituality. Having a small community of individuals working together with a common ideal in which to learn and express psychic ability is a great resource—a school of life in miniature. To be sure, this was one impetus that gave birth to Cayce's "A Search for God" Study Group program, as well as the associated Glad Helpers Prayer Group. The small group model, however, has also been used very effectively in the "Dream Helper Ceremony."

Growing out of psychologist Henry Reed's background in dreams and an understanding of Cayce's approach to intuition, the Dream Helper Ceremony has been repeatedly used at conferences, camp programs, dream seminars, and university settings. In this process, a group of three, four, or more individuals come together and agree to try to have dreams that are helpful to one of their group members. The person needing assistance has requested help but has kept secret what the nature of the problem actually is. Thus the group members' dreams have to be psychic on two levels: one, determining the nature of the problem; two, formulating a creative solution.

Group members may decide to surround the target person for a time of meditation and prayer. They can ask the target person to sign his or her name on enough index cards so that each participant can take one home to "dream on." Or the target person might instead decide to distribute some personal belongings to each "dreamer," such as jewelry, a comb, a key, and so forth. After the collective ceremony, each individual goes home and while falling asleep remembers that the goal is to dream for the person in need. Here the altruism helps not only the subconscious connection for identifying the problem but the universal consciousness level for coming up with creative solutions. The next day, group members gather and share their dreams. The process is to look for similar themes, images, and symbols in the dreams that may somehow reflect the target person's issue, as well as any possible suggestions.

Research by various folks in the Edgar Cayce community has repeatedly confirmed that this group project generally has constructive results, even among folks who are new to this area of study. What makes it a natural for psychic development is that in the dream state, the soul is the active consciousness. Working in a group with several dreams to explore for common elements provides a context for interpreting the dreams that would not otherwise be available when working alone. Since the dream can be interpreted for its meaning for the dreamer as well as for the person whom the dreamer hopes to help, the process helps build the sense of community and enhances the relationship between the persons. All of these developments are consistent with the soul's mission and embody a very constructive "psychic exercise."

Another very important aspect of the soul is its memory. We might say that the boundaries between souls are their choices, as our choices determine our experience and build our memories. Ultimately, our wisdom lies in what we've learned from our experiences. Thus each of our experiences can be a potential soul lesson—like a dream that can be interpreted for its lesson. Using memories, therefore, as a vocabulary to express spiritual wisdom, is an approach the soul can appreciate, and can also create an enlightening process to explore with a partner.

One person, we'll call this person the "seeker," sets a silent intention to receive a creative new perspective on some current personal challenge or dilemma. The other person, we'll call this person the "consultant," makes an attunement to the seeker, usually by imagining a heart connection, becoming as one. Then the consultant silently verbalizes an affirmation along these lines: "Please direct into my awareness a memory of a specific experience that I've had and which I can use as a metaphoric teaching story to express my creative perspective on my partner's unexpressed concern." The consultant accepts the first memory to come into awareness and tells that story to the seeker, not knowing the seeker's topic of concern. Through dialogue, connection, and empathy with one another, some interesting experiences in intuition and processing solutions result, truly demonstrating the truth of "psychic is of the soul."

This memory game is also a perfect process for self-exploration. Such a mission might be as follows: "What memory from a past experience can help me better understand and relate to this experience [identifying a situation]?" Ideally, the method could be used to answer a question such as, "What memory from my past can I use as a teaching story for myself to provide me with a creative perspective on this job offer I just received?" Clearly, when the issue is known, as in this example, the person would logically go through past job experiences to evaluate the current prospects. That's a natural process that anyone in that situation would go through, whether or not they formally posed the question to themselves as written here. The challenge to developing mission exercises involving intuition or psychic perception for oneself is that, knowing the question and one's own situation, one can bring all kinds of thoughts and assumptions to the question, posing as psychic impressions. Also, working with self lacks the "magical phenomena" associated with working with others, and requires a dedication to the soul growth purpose behind the psychic development program. One way to get around this is to create a barrier between your conscious mind and the self-related targets you wish to perceive psychically. For example, over a period of a month, you might note on individual index cards various concerns, questions, and issues that you are dealing with in life. Then, after having created at least a couple dozen, you can then pick one at random, not look at it, but make a heart connection to it, and ask for a memory to help you understand this issue in a more constructive manner.

So often Cayce asked of an inquirer whether they were interested merely in creating a psychic "phenomenon," or were they motivated by the desire to become more aware of their soul and its relation to the Creator and other souls? Today, the scientific philosophy going by the name of "evolutionary enlightenment" proposes that consciousness is a living reality on the move, always evolving. It does so through having to deal with confronting problems, obstacles, and frustrations. These blocks stimulate creativity. Each happens for a purpose, at a time when there's a readiness to grow and evolve. This modern perspective fits perfectly with Cayce's view on the role of psychic ability in human experience, and how it is best engaged. Perhaps it is one of those areas where the injunction for the right hand to remain ignorant of what the left hand is doing is good advice here. Learning to be psychic intentionally depends more upon aligning with our own soul and our interconnectedness with others than upon mental processes to stimulate psychic functioning. While success in psychic development will no doubt have some positive impact on self-esteem, it is best approached with concern for the esteem of the whole. Psychic development is a part of the process of growing beyond our assumed boundaries to take up our rightful place as being a soul in relationship to others. We are moving toward recognizing our shared reality in consciousness.

19

Channeling Your Higher Self

ONE OF THE ULTIMATE GOALS PRESCRIBED BY THE CAYCE READINGS for all individuals is that the soul needs to be able to find creative expression by working cooperatively with the divine. Although a unique process for each individual, it invariably involves inspiration, creativity, and the expression of information and insight from one's Higher Self. On occasion, the readings used the word "channeling" to describe this process, but it is not the definition of channeling that relates to mediumship or surrendering the self to something outside; instead, it is a creative, cooperative partnership that calls upon the very best within the self to work in cooperation with the divine and through that process somehow bring *spirit* into the earth.

Perhaps one of the most straightforward ways you can channel your Higher Self right now is through the use of the imagination. As an example, for a few moments simply imagine a beautiful, wonderful world where everyone prospers in abundance and gets along fine with everyone else. What does that world look like to you? How does it feel to be a part of that world? Next, imagine what you might do today—some good deed—that can contribute to that image and be in keeping with the wonderful world you've imagined. Then go do the deed! That's a great example of channeling your Higher Self.

The Cayce readings also provide another simple suggestion that can be practiced in the mornings upon awakening. Cayce told one woman to become quiet each morning and to ask the question, "Lord, what would you have me do today?" And then listen. By setting herself aside and being receptive to the answer, this process could enable her Higher Self to work creatively and cooperatively with the divine. That is what channeling your Higher Self is all about.

Hearing about these simple approaches, you might wonder, what about a trance? What about the amazing displays of transcendental consciousness coming through the person not from the person? What about spirit guides, angels, or galactic intelligence? Isn't that what channeling is all about? Isn't that what Cayce did?

Channeling can certainly involve these spectacles; however, such phenomena are but the tip of the iceberg. Those aspects of channeling that attract the most attention actually camouflage the most significant and profound meaning of channeling. Cayce's unique demonstrations of the far reaches of the mind have had a tremendous effect upon our vision of what's possible. His frequent use of the phrase "to become a channel of blessings" created a powerful image for connecting with transcendental or spiritual dimensions to pass along help and assistance to others. Today there are healers who channel intelligent energy in performing seemingly miraculous operations. Books, magazines, and especially the Internet provide "channeled" messages aplenty, including daily blogs of communication from "other realms" with counsel for us during times of challenge and change. Yet these manifestations do not necessarily reflect what Cayce had in mind when he encouraged us to become channels of blessings.

If the secret power of channeling does not lie in the depth of the trance or in the power of the spirit guide that we can get to come through, then where does the power lie? Edgar Cayce provides an overarching vision of our relationship to creation, the Creative Forces, and the Creator. To harness the true, creative, healing, inspirational power of channeling the Higher Self, one must become attuned and focused on the entire circle of relationships involved in the channeling process. Once again, a major Cayce theme comes into play: honoring our relationships.

Think of the cycle of exchanges that make up life. The sunlight comes upon the plants—that dance to make food that grows other life. We breathe in oxygen and exhale carbon dioxide, the complementary opposite to the plants' process. We channel the air we breathe and the food we eat into cultural items—clothing, housing, behaviors, and expressions. Channeling, in the sense of a circular linkage of relationships that transform patterns of energy into manifestation and keep the energy flowing, is everywhere and occurs always. Channeling the "higher self" then means that the ideal and purpose that are set involve the best interests of the greatest number of positive relationships and have a practical purpose of serving those interests.

There are two basic operative principles to understand. The first has to do with the access of information and inspiration—set your intent, then "watch yourself go by," as Cayce would describe that practice of specially prepared improvisation. The second has to do with the handling of that bounty—"use what you have in hand and more will be given," as Cayce often reminded.

To access inspiration from the Higher Self, begin by setting your intention. This attunement process is the most important part, with the greatest leverage, and involves both understanding your ideal and your purpose. It is in the realm of ideals that the higher consciousness exists—"higher" meaning values that connect with, honor, and nurture the entire web of creation. Having a constructive purpose in mind, and a genuine readiness to serve that purpose, completes that process of preparatory attunement.

After the attunement, whether it is during a sitting meditation or one done while dancing, comes the harvesting of the inspiration. Watching self go by—the creative improvisation part—is perhaps the most challenging. It is something that often tempts us to "leave the building" during the session in an attempt to "get out of our own way." It is not necessary for the ego to be absent itself during channeling (as in going unconscious during hypnosis-induced channeling and having amnesia for the session). If you're frustrated in your attempt to set self aside, to get out of your own way, that's natural. That's why the history of humankind contains many examples of the attempt to "knock oneself out," by hypnotic trance, drugs, strangulation, or starvation, to rid oneself of the interfering, control-freak of the conscious ego, so that the "good stuff" could come through.

Cayce's attitude toward unconscious channeling is something like: Well, if that's all you want, to get the answer, to prove your ability, that's fine. But if you'd like to learn how to grow into your Higher Self, why send your ego out of the classroom every time the higher self is about to appear?

It helps to keep the ego in the classroom while the lesson is presented, so it can also learn how to relax and become transparent to the silent witness. Your breathing can train your ego to become transparent. The word "inspiration" refers also to breathing. That natural process is the source of some of our intuitions about inner guidance. It also provides a simple way to practice "watching self go by." Observe your breath with these affirmations: "I can be aware of my breathing and let it be"; "I'm learning how to let go and let Spirit (Life, God) breathe me"; and "I'm learning to let go as the air flows out and to trust the inspirations."

In the next stage of the channeling cycle, we evaluate, test, or apply what came through during the session. We use the feedback to help us refine our understanding and to recalibrate our efforts. To express this part of the process in Cayce's own terms, it would be "... use what you have, and more will be given, for it is in the application that the awareness comes."

Perhaps the most common missing link in the channeling cycle is something we might call "grounding." Just as Benjamin Franklin found that lightning was electricity, because his kite from earth provided a "ground" for the lightning, when we channel, if we wish to bring down lightning, we must have grounding. What is the importance of this grounding? To provide a relationship that will continue the flow of energy, the development of the awareness through testing and application, and that will meet a need or serve a purpose in the world. Doing something only for sport, for show, or to prove something, excites the channel but does not create the complete circuit that a creatively functioning channel requires. A smile has a long effect, because its positive energy gets passed along. Native Americans call it "growing corn." Along with Edgar Cayce, that indigenous tradition recognized our human role as a nurturer, caretaker, and participant in the creative process of life.

To give grounding to these principles, let's examine what Cayce called "inspirational writing." He recommended it as a good place to begin.

He also noted that it had no limit for what good it could bring into the world. We can use it and understand the challenges involved, suggested strategies, and possible outcomes that arise in the various other modes of channeling. (Two influential examples of this form of channeling are the books *A Course in Miracles* and *Conversations with God*.)

Inspirational writing is spontaneous and free-flow. It is writing from the heart, from the spirit of the ideal set. Cayce distinguishes this form of channeled writing from what he calls the "automatic" type. The inspired writer is aware of what is being written, while the automatic writer is otherwise preoccupied and unaware of what is being written. It's the difference between purposeful and prepared improvisational writing and unconscious writing. In the former, we are conscious of our writing, but it seems as if it flows on its own rather than us making it up and recording it. To be able to "watch self go by" and not step in and direct the process requires practice.

It's a simple process. Try it first when confronting a simple dilemma, like what's most important to do or remember today? Prepare yourself by bringing pen and paper, or keyboard, close by to where you sit and meditate, or where you will do your preparation, whatever form it takes. Set the intent that at the end of the preparation, you will begin to write. One can begin by simply writing what you are feeling or experiencing at that moment, and let the writing flow out of itself. Afterwards, study the contents for a plan, for a way to apply an idea in what was written, such as how to spend your day. Follow through on the plan and repeat the process the next day.

Trust is an important part of the process. We must learn to trust that the information that comes through is worth exploring. If we expect that channeled material should arrive in finished form, with specific formulas, and certified extra-sensory information, we can be disappointed. But if we examine the material faithfully, finding in it something we can try out, often the discouraging words turn into a surprisingly useful guidance when applied.

Working in a group is also an important ingredient for learning to channel the higher self. It helps build trust in the process. Often we do not recognize the value of our inspired writing, because we are expecting something else or expression in a different form than our own—don't judge it by the handwriting! Research conducted by the

Edgar Cayce Institute for Intuitive Studies (ECIIS) demonstrated the value of working in a group in this way: The group decides upon both a method and a purpose for an experiment in channeling. It could be, for example, to use inspirational writing to provide guidance for one of the group members concerning an issue that is currently undisclosed. After a period of meditation to attune to the ideal of loving service, with the sense of a heart connection to that group member, the writing begins. Group members won't necessarily recognize the help that is in their writing, because they do not know the person's concern. But as the group members read their writing aloud, and hear what came through the other members, and then listen to the feedback provided by the recipient of all this guidance, it begins to dawn on folks that each person connected meaningfully with the hidden focus. It is the common themes that help them identify the message channeled in their writings.

Once the essential principles of channeling are digested, there are an infinite number of ways to engage the process. The book *Edgar Cayce on Channeling Your Higher Self* is an excellent resource in this regard. One of the least known of Cayce's suggestions about channeling has to do with art. In his descriptions of a historic Temple Beautiful in Egypt, where initiates had all their senses stimulated in pleasing ways, Cayce noted that aesthetic experience can attune us to spiritual awareness.

Experiments in conscious extemporaneous expression (creative improvisation) conducted by ECIIS explored the use of aesthetics. For an induction to an idealized state of consciousness, participants danced, or moved (or, in some cases, imagined dancing) to Strauss' The Blue Danube waltz, as Cayce recommended this music for its harmonizing effects. As to purpose, in one series of experiments, participants dedicated their writing to speak to a common concern, such as learning to trust within, how to set self aside, etc. After the moving attunement, participants did inspirational writing and shared the results aloud with the group.

Another series of experiments used this same method to explore intuitive dream interpretation. Each participant made an audio recording of a dream. Afterwards, they moved to the music of the The Blue Danube. When the music had finished, each person took someone else's audio recorded dream, listened to that dream, and then began inspirational writing with the purpose of providing useful information to the dreamer. Afterwards, the dreamers received back their dreams and the writing that their recorded dream inspired. Folks felt that surprising insights into themselves that came through the dreams were opened up by these "improvised comments" in the writing, which were judged to be authentic "blessings."

Given a most general view of the "channeling paradigm" as Cayce envisioned it: spiritually prepared (with varying degrees of alteration of consciousness) and with practical purpose, engaging in a process of creative improvisation to manifest something desired that is new, workable, and consistent with one's spiritual ideals. Then there are limitless styles of and arrangements and uses for channeling the higher self. There are as many purposes as there are human conditions and needs.

James Turrell, an American artist and student of the Edgar Cayce information, had in his dreams experiences of light and of becoming light. He worked for years to develop a way to create this light experience in viewers, exploring different ways of making an effective light projector. As a MacArthur Foundation "Genius" award–winning artist, his light sculptures around the world have been introducing people to the experience of the "light within." His project of reshaping an extinct volcano in Arizona to become a light reflector is the largest art project in history. Ultimately, channeling your Higher Self is about learning to engage with and live cooperatively with the divine spirit.

As a final example, here's a suggestion for an experiment in channeling that expresses Cayce's vision of the ideal spiritual cycle of soul growth through service to others. Upon awakening in the morning, adopt a meditative frame of mind, and then ask, "What experience will I encounter today that will provide me with an opportunity to discover and apply an unrealized soul ability by helping someone I meet?" Take whatever information that comes through, keep it in mind during the day, and watch for that opportunity. Explore this process for a few weeks, keeping a journal, and you'll begin to realize that we are always being guided, whether we are aware of it or not, to step up to being our higher self and sharing the blessing with others.

There is no limit on the amount or kind of blessings that we can share with others through this practice. The process enables us to move beyond the confines of what we may think we know about ourselves, and our perception of limitations, and instead engage in a cooperative creation, becoming a "channel of blessings" to someone in need. Edgar Cayce, in his own experiences with personal growth, and the aspirations he had for us, felt that channeling one's higher self was a wonderful method of helping others and becoming aware of our divine self. Learning to channel blessings for others as a means of coming to realize our own co-creative abilities with God is the ultimate purpose for learning the skill of channeling your Higher Self.

20

Understanding Disturbing Psychic Experiences

ONE PREMISE CONTAINED WITHIN THE EDGAR CAYCE READINGS IS that there is a purposefulness entailed within even the most problematic or disturbing psychic experience. This may come as a surprise to some who have had these kinds of incidents, as they are generally upsetting, often overwhelming, and frequently seem totally disconnected from the individual having the experience. However, the readings suggest that not only are there reasons that these experiences occur, but they are also thematically and symbolically connected to the viewer. Cayce indicated that all dreams, visions, and other psychic phenomena arise for a reason. Each has its purpose, which could be discovered, would the person spend the time investigating the experience.

Modern research has confirmed Cayce's suggestion as to the purposefulness of many spontaneous psychic experiences. For example, Louisa Rhine, the wife of J.B. Rhine, inventor of statistical ESP research, compiled several books from letters she received. In such titles as *Hidden Channels of the Mind*, she noted the apparent purposefulness of many of these experiences. Premonitions of visitors, romance, pregnancies, births, and deaths were common themes in these stories. Anthropologists studying indigenous peoples found similar themes, with the addition of themes related to hunting and weather. Such premonitions seem natural, as they help prepare folks for what is coming. Cayce indicated, in fact, that anything of importance that happens to us is previewed in a dream, helping us, at some level (remembered or not) to prepare ourselves.

Sometimes the psychic experience goes unnoticed, blending in with ongoing thought. Charles Thomas Cayce, a psychologist and grandson of Edgar Cayce, tells the story of being surprised by the results of his participation in an ESP laboratory experiment. The researchers asked Charles Thomas to write on ten index cards ten names of people he knew. After taking the cards, the researcher attached an electrode to Charles Thomas's wrist to measure sweating, similar to a lie detector. Charles Thomas was told that the experiment would start shortly and he was left alone to sit in the room. In another room, an assistant wrote ten random names from the phone book on ten cards. The assistant shuffled those ten with the ten cards that Charles Thomas had contributed, and began to read aloud, one at a time, each name. Meanwhile, the element attached to Charles Thomas's wrist recorded the level of moisture on his wrist. Although he was unaware of what was happening, not even knowing that the experiment was already underway, every time the assistant read aloud a name of someone Charles Thomas knew, the recorder showed a small spike in his sweat response. There was no such spike when the assistant read the names of people unknown to Charles Thomas. There have been many such studies conducted demonstrating what researchers call "unconscious ESP." The implication is that you can be psychically affected by someone else without even realizing it. Having a sudden onset of troubling emotions could be one sign of such an effect. If there's nothing a person can do with such experiences, what purpose could they possibly serve?

As with all experience, Cayce would say that we are meeting self. Our experience is a mirror reflecting ourselves. The purpose of the experience is to help us grow in the awareness of our oneness with the Creator so that we might live in co-creative companionship. If disturbing psychic experiences are a part of the mix of purposeful events, how are we to integrate them?

Edgar Cayce provided two elementary principles to explain the occurrence and content of disturbing, unwanted psychic experiences. The first had to do with what we might call a breakdown in a boundary. For some, he described a breakdown in the functioning of one of the psychic centers. This could be caused by a physical trauma. In his own case, for example, as a youth, getting hit in the head with a baseball had the effect of awakening some psychic experiences. This kind of psychic-prompting trauma could also be emotional, resulting from physical, psychological, or verbal abuse. Taking someone's judgment to heart could also create a hole in the aura, as it were, for now something alien to the person has penetrated the person's sense of self. In addition to mental, emotional, and physical trauma, ways of breaking down the aura can include alcohol, drug, or other substance abuse.

Once the breakdown has occurred, one of the first steps to regaining psychic protection and a restoration of personal boundaries is to restore one's integrity (wholeness). A first important principle to keep in mind regarding the restoration of integrity is to recall that we are spiritual beings endowed by the Creator with free will. Ultimately, nothing is more powerful than our own will. Nothing can overcome our will without our giving permission, however indirect. When we take a criticism to heart, for example, we are accepting it. It's good to be able to learn from criticism, but if we overdo it, it harms our sense of self.

To restore this integrity, one must exercise one's free will to bolster one's natural defenses and to affirm that one can choose not to be responsive to the disturbing psychic influence. How do you exercise this act of free will to make it effective? At a physical level, a chiropractic or osteopathic adjustment may correct any spinal contribution to this unwanted "opening." It is also important to eat well-balanced meals and, especially, not to go hungry, because this state of depletion makes a person more vulnerable. At a mental level, reading inspirational literature is helpful. Spiritually, prayer is very beneficial, as it helps you to affirm your essential connection with the divine. For some, an essential step is to examine oneself to be sure that there is no fascination with the "psychic." Psychic ability doesn't need to be shut off, but it is more constructive when it operates within our intentions and ideals. When affirming one's free will and choice to be at peace seems to be insufficient to stop the unwanted phenomena, it is necessary to dig deeper, applying Cayce's second principle, regarding the meaning for self of the content of the experience.

One example is the story of Jack. He met a man at a weekend work-shop, and this man's mysterious ways fascinated him for days later. One night, Jack awoke in the middle of the night feeling that the man was in the room. It seemed like nonsense, yet the feeling that the man was somehow close by was very strong. Jack could "feel" his presence. He began to sense that this man "knew" where Jack was, and was in mental contact with him. Jack was worried, as the tone was menac-ing, as if this man had evil, even murderous thoughts about Jack. He recalled Cayce's principle of the impenetrability of our free will, and so he affirmed that he chose not to meet self via an encounter with this man; that he chose to meet this aspect of self in meditation. He found peace in the meditation, and as he came out of it, he realized that the part of himself that he subconsciously recognized in this man was a tendency toward self-destruction. Jack surveyed some of the ways he had been self-destructive, and processed some of his feelings about himself. Thoughts of this man never returned, except for Jack's being grateful that he'd had this learning opportunity.

Jack's experience brings us to the second part of Cayce's approach to such experiences. Since everything we experience is a meeting of self, then the content of the disturbing psychic experience must be reflect-ing one's self in some manner. In Jack's case, for example, the destruc-tiveness he feared from this man was a reflection of self-destructive tendencies in Jack that were ready to enter into his awareness. These are learning opportunities.

Cayce used the term "affinity" to explain the source of unwanted psychic experiences. Whether we use the term "law of attraction," or "like attracts like," "resonance," or "affinity," we need to understand that the content of the experience is potentially revealing about the per-son having the experience. Like a dream, such an experience can be interpreted, for it is happening for a reason. It is like a wake-up call to awaken people to their abilities or to heal a past wound; or part of a transformation process—a rebirthing into a more spiritual sense of self. Probing these experiences for their underlying meaning is a worthwhile challenge. No matter what the content of the experience, it reflects selective attention. Why dream of a natural disaster and not of a corporation going bankrupt? Why dream of something terrible when there are good things happening? What is behind the choice of disturbing psychic experiences?

Another example of working with an unwanted psychic experience occurred to a woman named Nancy. Nancy awoke one morning having had a nightmare about a dog finding a young infant girl lying in a remote part of a forest battered to death. As part of an Atlantic University project, Nancy was assigned a student as a "buddy" with whom to coordinate daily simultaneous meditations. The students combined two of Edgar Cayce's suggestions to create an experiment to see if it would be possible to help people like Nancy. At the conclusion of each meditation, the student and the "psychic buddy" would tune into each other for any psychic impressions. Once a week, they would have a telephone conversation, share their impressions, and get feedback. The student working with Nancy kept track of the kinds of information Nancy received about the student. It was a means of assessing the themes and topics for which Nancy seemed to have selective attention. As their experiment proceeded, Nancy became aware of some dark memories from her childhood. Ultimately, Nancy realized that she had repressed memories of abuse and that her disturbing psychic experience was somewhat like what the psychiatrist Sigmund Freud called "the return of the repressed." Her disturbing psychic experience was her attempt to bring to awareness painful memories that needed healing. At this realization, her concern over disturbing psychic experiences vanished, and she began to use her abilities for personal guidance.

Remember the Challenger disaster? Many people had documented precognitive dreams about it. Why did some folks dream of it while others did not? In another project, conducted at the ECIIS, two people who had had such dreams participated. A group of psychics were asked to interpret each of these two people's dreams, not knowing the actual content or their relationship to the Challenger disaster. In each case, the dream interpretations the psychics provided revealed personal connections between the dreamers and aspects of the Challenger problem. Doris, like one of the doomed astronauts, was a teacher. Like the teacher astronaut, Doris had also taken some risks, and although she had not died, she had truly suffered for some things she attempted. In fact, she felt "shot down" at school. Tony, a bit of a rebel, had been fired from his job for criticizing the way things were run. Somewhat of a whistleblower, he had uncovered unethical and unsafe practices at his job, and his reward was being fired. As the investigation of the Challenger disaster unfolded, the drama of the engineers' warning about potential trouble, and the administration's ignoring of those warnings in order to meet performance deadlines, echoed Tony's experience at work. For both these people, the Challenger disaster was a deeply soul-stirring event that resonated with personal tragedies and malfeasance they had experienced. In both cases, each felt a bit of vindication by the public outcry and grief over the disaster.

Often, the ability to stand back from the experience and contemplate its nature or source is helpful. In the case of emotional contagion, or having a sudden attack of strong feelings, one might ask oneself, Whose feelings are these? Sometimes mindfulness can provide an answer.

Another example occurred in the case of John. John's meditation was suddenly interrupted one day by intense feelings of resentment against his dentist. He got so upset he had to break off the meditation and go for a walk. As he cooled down, he wondered what could have triggered this disturbing replay of a past incident at the dentist's office. He assumed he'd let go of it. The thought of a male client came to mind, someone he had an appointment to counsel that evening, and John felt inexplicably calmed. Later that evening, during their counseling session, the client told John about how his wife and a tenant had both abused him by taking advantage of his good nature. Although it was clear that the client felt hurt, angry, and taken for granted, his voice was calm and without a hint of emotion. John, on the other hand, was feeling the agitation of righteous indignation. He realized he was literally feeling the client's anger, doing the feeling for the client, because the client was cut off from his own feelings. At that moment, John realized why he had been so upset earlier in the day during meditation. He had found himself thinking about how the dentist had convinced him, against his own wishes, to have a certain treatment. He had gone along reluctantly and then simply relegated the experience to a bad dentist memory—seemingly, no big deal. But as he listened to his client, he realized that he had not totally processed his experience. His psychic connection with the client had resurfaced his anger at the personal insult and humiliation he felt at being so easily manipulated by the dentist. His disturbing psychic experience was resonating with feelings that needed attention. When one has important issues that are not being addressed, sometimes a disturbing psychic experience can bring the matter to attention.

Edgar Cayce repeatedly emphasized the importance of the spiritual over the psychic. The latter is a function, a reality within the scheme of things, whereas the former is the purpose for our being here. The psychic, especially in the form of intuitive guidance, can serve the spiritual. Rather than becoming spiritual so we don't abuse the psychic, the ultimate reason spirituality is such an important prerequisite is that it can become overwhelming to be so aware of things. One has to grow into love, acceptance, non-judgment, compassion, and so on, before one can handle experiencing and knowing the various dimensions of the human experience. Are you ready to remember all your soul memories? Can you view your past mistakes with compassion? Can you accept other people's limitations with good humor? Can you learn to love each individual the way that God loves that individual—in spite of his or her shortcomings?

We are destined to become aware of, and co-responsible for, all of creation. Unwanted psychic experiences are invitations to expand one's awareness. They are wakeup calls—gifts. Yet they require loyalty to the ideal of consciousness and the willingness to look in the mirror. Even disturbing experiences are part of the Creator's plan for our personal and collective growth and awakening.

21

Dreaming for Guidance

ONE OF THE MOST PRACTICAL AND HELPFUL PRINCIPALS CONTAINED IN the work of Edgar Cayce is the fact that each and every one of us has a potentially limitless source of guidance and counsel readily available to us in our dreams. Dreams can give accurate insights into every area of life—even things of which we have no conscious awareness. The guidance available in dreams can provide insight into any question and life issue we are facing: our health and physical wellbeing, our work and relationships, our emotional and psychological concerns, spiritual and soul growth issues—even our futures—as well as matters beyond our personal concern, such as revelations about the nature of reality!

Almost 900 of the 14,306 readings in the Cayce archives deal with the topic of dreams and dream interpretation. Most often, Gertrude (Cayce's wife), would hold the written dream in her hand and ask for an interpretation—without the dream ever being read! More amazing still, on several occasions when asked for an interpretation, Cayce would comment that the dreamer had forgotten a portion of her or his dream and provide the missing details along with an overall interpretation.

Cayce was one of the first individuals in the West to recommend that all people learn to work with their dreams and perhaps the very first to give them the tools to do so. Today, dream study is more common, with a growing resource of teachers of dream interpretation. Cayce consistently recommends comparative study, and exploring the similarities and differences in these new dream work approaches would be no exception. His perspective, however, takes us beyond the need for such external teachers and their systems. He proposes we discover that our own dreams can teach us how to gain guidance from them. The key is our intention to follow through and our actual readiness to apply the insights the dreams suggest.

Hundreds of individuals proved Cayce's proposition in a history-making experiment. Using a simple "Dream Solutions" workbook prepared for this project that contained step-by-step instructions, folks recorded and worked with their dreams for 28 days. The purpose of this "dream quest" was to collaborate with one's dreams to make meaningful progress on some personal issue or creative project. On a weekly cycle, participants would examine their dreams for insights, develop a plan to test or apply the insights in the coming week, and then assess the next batch of dreams for progress.

Here's an example of this process, from a woman who later published her story about how her dream quest helped her improve her relationship with her daughter. Her first week of dreams pointed to her daughter as a major concern. For the next week, she applied an insight from those dreams that she consider her own spiritual ideal by daily reminder and journaling. The second week's dream collection inspired the woman to practice in all her relations the attitude she wished to have with her daughter. During the third week, her daughter called her—for the first time in a long while—just to visit. By the end of her dream quest, this woman had a revitalized relationship with her daughter and a new-found method of meditation and prayer.

The results of the experiment generally were quite encouraging, with one statistical observation especially worth noting: It turned out that applying a dream insight had a powerful effect on subsequent dreams, more powerful than meditation! It was the first public demonstration of the self-educating power of dreams and played a role in the development of the overall public interest in dreams and the creation of the International Association for the Study of Dreams. Their work awakened the world to the power of dreams that is within reach of everyone. It also demonstrated that this power had virtually no limits—what might be the implications of a culture that honored dreams?

Dream guidance can be amazingly psychic. Consider the story of a woman in Australia. She had a series of very serious complaints that had gone on for years: dizziness, fainting spells, stomach and liver problems, frequent exhaustion, gas pains, and problems with her digestion. After having been to many doctors without success, a member of her Edgar Cayce study group suggested that she pray for dream guidance as to what she was supposed to do about her situation. A few nights later she had a dream. In the dream she was looking at an Edgar Cayce reading that was numbered "1880."

As this was in the 1970s, before home computers or the Internet, a letter was written to A.R.E. in Virginia Beach, Va., asking for a copy of the reading numbered 1880, which was then sent to her. When she received it in the mail, she was astounded, as the reading described her symptoms exactly! This health reading had been given to a 54-year-old man in 1939, who had asked about the very same health issues she was exhibiting. He had been diagnosed with mercury poisoning.

The woman then asked her mother if she could have gotten mercury poisoning as a child. Her mother informed her that when she had been a young girl, she had bitten off the end of a thermometer and swallowed the contents. As a result, the woman asked her doctor to test her for mercury poisoning. The results were positive. She followed the same advice Cayce had given the individual almost 40 years earlier, which included a complete change in diet and internal and external medications, and within four months, she returned to perfectly normal health!

How can dreams get such information? The answer lies in the nature of the mind. In fact, Cayce had a dream about it! In his dream, he saw the mind as a giant star, radiating pointed shafts of light. The endpoints of the shafts represented our individual, conscious sensory minds. Just behind the point lies the subconscious mind closest to awareness. All shafts are connected with each other, making it possible for one subconscious mind to communicate with another. At the center of the star is the superconscious mind, which contains the universal intelligence and patterns of creation, all knowledge, realized or not. His dream was a perfect example of what it expressed about the superconscious mind—a deep knowledge of the secrets of creation.

Another aspect of the mind illustrated in this dream is the relation-ships between the levels of the mind. One of the interesting things about the conscious, sensory mind is that it filters out its awareness of most of the information and stimulus coming to it. We are generally not aware of such things as the feeling of the clothing on our body, the sensation of the glasses on our nose, the watch on our wrist, the ring on our finger, our feet on the floor, the sounds of the heating and air conditioning system, the intensity of the light in a room, the noise being made by a coworker sitting near us—most things around us—unless we draw our attention to them. This holds true for all of our subtle inter-actions with people and events. And yet, all of these things that pass unrecognized and unaware through the sensory mind reside within the realm of the subconscious mind and are brought to the surface in dreams. In fact, the amazing storehouse of the subconscious mind is the very reason that individuals can often remember more that went on at a crime scene under hypnosis, for example, than they remember consciously. It is the subconscious mind that awakens while we sleep, providing dreamers with insights and guidance about their bodies, their minds, and even their souls, as well as the world around them and its secrets.

In terms of the physical guidance that can be obtained in dreams, these are dreams that can deal with our health, our physical well-being, even suggestions for dealing with illness and disease. One ex-ample from Cayce's own life occurred when he had been suffering for an extended period with a severe cough and cold. One night during the illness, he had a dream in which he seemed to be mixing various ingredients (including boiling water, honey, syrup, glycerin, whiskey, etc.) in specific measurements for a medicine for him to take. Upon awakening, he prepared the formula he had dreamed about and found relief from his cough and cold.

Another example of physical guidance in dreams occurred in the life of a business professional more than thirty years after a high school football injury. At the time of the incident, there had been minor inter-nal injuries to his hip, but he thought nothing more of the problem for several decades until he began having alternate "numb and throbbing" pains near the area of the original problem. One night a dream seemed to provide the prognosis: "A female surgeon is in a hospital room examining me. After examining me, she looks up, touches the area of my hip and says, 'There's no longer any doubt, this has got to come out.'" The dream prompted the businessman to make an appointment with his doctor, who referred him to a surgeon. After examining the hip, the surgeon recommended and then performed surgery to remove old scar tissue and the remnants of internal bleeding that had occurred decades previously. After the surgery and his recovery, the dreamer was no longer bothered by the pain in his hip.

In terms of emotional or psychological guidance, during a period when Edgar Cayce had been very worried about his personal finances and whether or not enough people would come to him for readings, enabling him to support his family, he had a dream. In the dream he seemed to be walking along a Paris street scene with the Duke and Duchess of Windsor (at the time, obviously a symbol of wealth) and Jesus! As they were walking along, Cayce suggested to his companions that they stop at one of the sidewalk cafés and enjoy a glass of champagne. As soon as they sat down, Cayce was frustrated with himself and wondered why he had invited everyone as he only had three pennies in his pocket. Nonetheless, they had their champagne and then the Duke and Duchess got up to leave. Worried about what he was supposed to do next, as he had no money to pay the bill, Cayce looked about nervously. In response, Jesus clapped his hands together in joy, started laughing, and asked: "Will I have to send you after a fish too?" The reference was obviously to Matthew 17:24–27 when Jesus sent several Apostles to catch a fish that had a coin stuck in its mouth--the very amount they needed to pay a tax. Obviously, the dream was suggesting that Cayce simply needed to have the faith that his needs would be met.

In terms of spiritual and soul guidance or visionary experiences, Cayce suggested that this is often the level where intuitive experiences can occur. On one occasion, Gladys Davis had a dream experience that seemed to foretell the future. She had been visiting a Mr. and Mrs. Ladd for the weekend on Long Island in New York. That evening, Mrs. Ladd told her about her husband's financial difficulties and the fact that he was about to lose his job. That night, Gladys remembers getting into bed wishing she could do or say something to help. She had a dream in which she saw Mr. Ladd, who always dressed as a businessman, wearing a lumber jacket, holding a coal scuttle in his hand, enter into the room she was sleeping in (a cottage in the dream), and tell her he was warming up her room. She thought nothing of the dream upon awakening. However, more than a year later while she was staying on a farm in New Jersey, she was awakened one morning with a knock on her door. She said "come in" and, according to Gladys, "there stood Mr. Ladd in his lumber jacket, a coal bucket in his hand, and he said, 'I thought you'd like to have a little fire in your stove to take the chill off while you get dressed.' I immediately noticed that the little room was exactly the same as I had dreamed it over a year ago."

Amazed by the accuracy of her dream, Gladys asked in a reading as to how this was even possible, to which Cayce replied: " ... as thought and purpose and aim and desire are set in motion by minds, their effect is as a condition that *is* . . . [the] *dream* is but *attuning* an individual mind to those individual storehouses of experience that has been set in motion . . . " (262–83) On other occasions, Cayce told individuals that precognitive guidance occurs in dreams because, by being "forewarned," the dreamer was better able to respond to the situation.

To see how easy it is to get a dream of guidance, researchers at Harvard University encouraged students to dream about some personal concern. They found that the topics of health and the body stimulated the most recognizable dream responses. Symbols of houses, plumbing, wiring, and other aspects of one's "dwelling" were common. In contrast to our previous examples, dreams of guidance are not always so literally explicit, but make use of parable, metaphor, and personal associations.

One of Cayce's most important principles, therefore, for interpreting dreams is, "correlate those truths." It means finding a correspondence between something happening in the dream and something happening in one's life. It is an intuitive process, as the cultural philosopher Gregory Bateson noted, intuition is seeing "the pattern that connects."

As an example, whatever emotion is being aroused within the dream generally corresponds to a situation or experience in the dreamer's waking life that evokes a similar feeling or emotion. For example, a person dreamed of driving in her car on her way to work when she had to stop at a red light. As the light turned green, she started to enter the intersection when another car, coming from her right, ran the red light. She stopped just in time to avoid a collision. Shaken, she proceeded on her way.

What is a "truth" displayed in this dream? One truth might be, "someone avoids an unfortunate event by paying attention." Another might be, "having to respond to an unanticipated danger provokes strong feelings." When the dreamer thought about the connections between each of these truths and what was going on with her life, she realized that she was being warned not to take for granted her boss's flattery, so that she could respond more gracefully upon an unwanted advance.

As a general principal, it pays to correlate truths from several sources, as this final dream story will show. When some adults and children got together to discuss dreams at Edgar Cayce's A.R.E. Camp in Rural Retreat, Va., they discovered something important that led to the creation of a unique educational tool—direct from dreams—that has since helped many people around the world experience for themselves the value and power of dreams. The children relayed stories about dreams that they had had concerning their friends that proved to be true. One of the adults had also had many such dream experiences and was able to help the children appreciate this way of understanding ourselves through our relationships. One of the other adults had previously dreamed a special "visionary" dream when he first visited A.R.E. in Virginia Beach, Va.:

"We are gathered together for research into enlightenment, but we don't know how to begin. We are in the dark and are stumbling about, bumping into each other. Suddenly, we begin to dance together in a circle. Each person displays a personal symbol by which the others recognize some truth. As they dance, a fountain of sparks erupt from the center, providing an umbrella of light around them. They realize, 'This is the way to conduct our research!'"

Using this visionary dream to connect the campers' dream experiences of their friends, they attempted a new experiment at camp. Campers who were experiencing some crisis at home volunteered to be the focus of the dreams for a small group of other campers. These other campers, without knowing anything about the volunteer's personal issue, promised to remember a dream for this person. The next day, the dreamers shared their dreams with the focus person. Although they knew very little of dream psychology, they followed Cayce's principle of correlating truths by examining the commonalities among the group's dreams. All during this discussion they remained in the dark about the focus person's issue. The focus person, facing away from the group during their discussion, had listened intently but silently. At the end of the discussion, the focus person responded to the dreams and their discussion. To the campers' surprise and delight, the focus person was very enthusiastic about the information that came out of the discussion.

This unusual experiment came to be given the name, "The Dream Helper Ceremony." At first, the name meant to imply how the volunteer was helped by the dreams. However, more was to come. In the decades since it was first conducted, researchers from various universities (Saybrook University, Columbia University, and the University of Florida) have conducted and made important observations about similar experiments. For one, it stimulates people to remember their dreams, confirming Cayce's belief that the main reason for lack of dream recall is negligence. For another, it does stimulate dreams that are meaningful to the volunteer person, often containing explicit psychic information about the volunteer. At the same time, echoing Cayce's premise that all dreams have some element reflective of self, another stimulating aspect is that each dreamer can also find a personal connection with the volunteer, as their dream also reflects a related truth about the dreamer. So it enhances a sense of empathy within the group as it teaches them a bit about dream psychology. This latter educational aspect supports Cayce's proposition that the best place to learn about dreams is in a small group.

Ultimately, however, everyone can gain a wealth of guidance, information, and insight from their own dreams. Perhaps the most important tool is simply to begin working with your dreams. Begin by keeping track of your dreams, looking for associations with events and relationships in your waking life. Applying any dream insights you receive has been shown to lead to greater personal awareness.

Cayce contended that all dreams were for the benefit of the individual having them if she or he would simply begin to work with them. The awareness of the power of dreams has spread worldwide, encouraging countless individuals to acquire a source of enlightenment simply by remembering their dreams.

22

Prosperity and Economic Healing

EDGAR CAYCE LIVED DURING A TIME OF GREAT GLOBAL UNCERTAINTY. The Great Depression, personal and economic hardship, and the world at war were all common sources of anguish. People came to Edgar Cayce looking for help regarding their personal financial problems. They also sought guidance about finding a career and a life path that would provide greater economic certainty. They looked for assistance in dealing with personal debt. And, of course, they were afraid.

"How am I going to take care of my family?" "Where are we going to live?" "What am I supposed to be doing at this stage in my life?" "How can I pay these bills?" These are just some of the questions from a long list that the Cayce readings addressed. Whatever their source of fear—whether concerns about the future, worries over monetary problems, or fear resulting from any major personal challenge, such as the loss of a job—the readings contend that all of sources of fear work contrary to the flow of material resources. Nonetheless, we all have to deal with practical issues in the midst of economic challenges. Trying to respond with a spiritual approach to such practical concerns stimulated Cayce's source to provide a proven body of information that has helped countless individuals, even decades later. The information in the Cayce files on dealing with personal financial problems is about much more than money—it provides a practical lesson concerning our role of co-creation.

In the face of personal challenge, Edgar Cayce often encouraged individuals to begin to change their mindset, replacing the paralysis of fear and apprehension with an attitude of self-efficacy—believing "I can make a difference." Realizing we have a choice of response is to acknowledge our creative potential. He encouraged individuals to have faith and to use what they had in hand in order to draw to themselves additional opportunities and material resources. To put it into familiar terms, rather than focus on the emptiness in the glass, we must focus on even the smallest drop that might still exist and use it for something. The readings considered this change in mind set as "job one!"

The readings on personal economic healing provide a number of straightforward suggestions for beginning to improve your material well-being. These include working with spiritual ideals, practicing stewardship and personal tithing, becoming cognizant of personal lessons needed by the soul (and attempting to learn them), living your soul's purpose, and being of service to others.

During the 1940s, a group of Cayce enthusiasts from New York City began working with relevant concepts from the Cayce readings in a project to overcome the financial challenges that each of them had been experiencing. The group began working as essentially an economic healing "support group" and undertook a three-month program of prayer, meditation, working with spiritual principles, and improving attitudes and their relationships with others, as well as tithing money and time. Members of the group immediately recognized that their own economic problems were not linked to a lack of talent or potential but instead to other factors. For that reason, group members chose to begin applying spiritual principles to their material lives, while removing any of their own mental blocks regarding the challenges with their own finances.

The group's explorations applying Cayce's spiritual economic principles resulted in a manual and later expanded into a booklet. [Note: that information has since been incorporated into the Edgar Cayce series volume, *Spiritual Healing for Personal Prosperity*.] Countless groups and individuals over many decades have since used and validated its principles and practical applications; some of the strategies include the following:

- Daily prayer and meditation, not only to facilitate personal attunement and getting in touch with one's spiritual core but to also assist in overcoming any fear of lack. Personal attunement can also be instrumental in maintaining an awareness of the soul's co-creative purpose for being in the earth.
- Ongoing work with personal relationships—at home, school, and work—wherever they may be. Rather than seeing people as personal challenges that have to be put up with, the Cayce readings encourage us instead to approach all of our relationships with the ideal of, "What am I supposed to be learning from this person?" or "What is this person trying to teach me about myself?" Ultimately, the only person we can change is self, but as self begins to change, individuals around us begin to change in terms of how they respond to the person we are in the process of becoming.
- Being a good steward of the resources that have been entrusted to us. This includes paying bills promptly, not overspending or overindulging, and giving self the freedom to buy what is needed (although not necessarily everything that is wanted). It also embodies the spiritual law of tithing—giving out to others both money and time without thought of receiving something in return.
- Keeping an ongoing chart of progress. This chart may include everything from keeping track of our daily prayer and meditation time, to the timely success of paying bills and paying off any debts, to personal tithing, positive experiences with improving our relationships, and notations of any surprising economic assistance that has come along, and so forth.

Yet these practical things can hide the real spiritual adventure Cayce invited us to explore. That is to use material and economic challenges as aids and guides to spiritual growth and oneness with God. Although it can be exasperating to fully comprehend, the readings suggest that one important component of economic challenges is the idea that they are used as a means for the individuals to become cognizant of such things as: their connection to spirit, the importance of working in concert with the divine, and coming to an understanding of personal lessons needed by our souls for growth and development. They are particularly powerful because of our attachment to material security.

Edgar Cayce himself frequently had financial challenges. He often wondered where his next client for a reading was coming from, whether or not he would have enough resources to feed his family, and if he could pay the bills. However, his own readings suggested that if he would simply have the faith, his needs would always be met.

As one contemporary example, Alex had heard about the "economic healing" material in the Cayce readings and began working with tithing as a regular practice. He gave to various non-profits, activities, and individuals, oftentimes anonymously, without expecting anything in return. He adopted an international foster child as part of his tithing practice. He also joined a small study group that worked with the principles of economic healing that had been discussed by the first New York group. Eventually, life events caused him to be a little short of funds, but he continued his commitment to tithing nonetheless. One morning he woke up and opened his shaving drawer to get his razor, and to his astonishment, he found a $100 bill carefully folded and hidden under some of the other items in the drawer. Alex had no explanation for the find, and eventually decided that he must have tucked it in the drawer a couple of years earlier (something he had never remembered consciously doing), but the money was especially helpful at his own time of shortage. Time continued to pass and he was about to get married when suddenly he was faced with an unexpected expense of $700. In spite of the sum, which was quite a lot for his income, he continued to tithe, telling his bride-to-be about his dedication to "helping others" with tithing. To his surprise, at the wedding one of their mutual friends gave him an envelope with a check in it stating that the check was to help them out in their new life together. The amount of the check was exactly $700!

Prosperity seems to originate from within, but how does that pay the bills? Ideals are one of the most important practices that we can undertake to exact personal change, and such practice will have practical implications. Working with ideals creates a spiritual roadmap based upon our choice of guiding star. That roadmap entails an overreaching goal, attitudes and emotions that will facilitate an understanding of that goal, and activities that must be done to help stimulate the practical application of the roadmap/pathway we have chosen. A good way to use ideals to create a practical step forward is to ask oneself, "What might this spiritual figure (or person) do in a similar situation of economic challenge?" "How have others responded to problems of this nature?" "What thoughts can I dwell upon that will help co-create a solution rather than constantly rehash the problem?" And, perhaps most importantly, "What are some of the things I can do right now to help change the energy and move forward?"

Cayce often reminded individuals of economic healing principles from scripture, including this verse from Matthew, which is not an encouragement to sit idle and do nothing, but rather an admonition to make certain one's focus is in the appropriate direction:

> "Consider the lilies of the field, how they grow; they toil not, neither do they spin . . . Wherefore, if God so clothe the grass of the field, which today is, and tomorrow is cast into the oven, shall he not much more clothe you, O ye of little faith? Therefore take no thought, saying, What shall we eat? or, What shall we drink? or, Wherewithal shall we be clothed? . . . for your heavenly Father knoweth that ye have need of all these things. But seek ye first the kingdom of God, and his righteousness; and all these things shall be added unto you." (Matthew 6:28-33)

This reference to nature is an important clue to Cayce's approach to abundance, healing, and spirituality in general. Nature can be one of our greatest teachers, with appropriate lessons ready at hand. Being in fear over money, for example, results from the perception of separation. Nature has no separate parts and can teach us how to remember our inherent connection with the force of all life. The affirmation meditation on relaxing into the natural flow of the breath, "Life breathes me, and I am learning to trust inspiration," provides immediate relief and a chance to think and strategize while in a more parasympathetic state of mind. It also reminds us, in a very physical way, that Spirit is the source of life, and we can trust it. To let go of our effort to control the breathing, to actually feel the life-giving breath coming freely to the body, helps to remind us that just as the breath comes and goes, it maintains us in a relationship with the plants sharing life with us on the planet. And we remember that it is our relationships—our giving and receiving, our assimilating and elimination—that provides the actual channel of economic health.

As another example of nature's way inspiring means of economic vitality, consider Sally's story. Having been laid off from her job, she was spending free time in her garden, where she would meditate on ideas for a new life. As she was digging up last year's failed carrot crop, she realized it resulted from a lack of thinning. Stuff needs room to grow. Where was Sally crowded? Certainly her closet was overfull. She decided to prune her closet, giving to Goodwill any item of clothing that she had not worn in two years. She was surprised to discover how much "excess" clothing was jammed into her closet. Soon she was doing a super editing job on her belongings, getting rid of a lot of "stuff" from the past that no longer served her. During her several trips to Goodwill, she met a woman who reminded Sally of her interest in making little gifts from found objects. Not long after, Sally began to develop a small crafts business for herself, recycling objects from Goodwill into artsy little gifts. Her business gave her a satisfaction that had long been missing from her previous line of work.

As it relates to stewardship and tithing, the premise pointed out by the Cayce information is that ultimately everything is God's property. Obviously, this concept may come as a surprise to some when it is first encountered. Nevertheless, everything we think we possess is in fact lent to us by God for the purpose of stewardship and service. On a number of occasions, individuals who received counsel from Cayce were informed that forgetting, ignoring, or remaining ignorant of this premise was one of the reasons they were having challenges in their personal finances. It may be important to note that we are not asked to give everything we have away; instead, we are encouraged to become cognizant of the fact that personal success is best measured in terms of how we use our success to assist others. In terms of actually giving away money and donating to other causes or individuals, Cayce specifically recommended giving a tithe of ten percent to charity, service activities, or to someone in need. Along these lines, another very important component of both stewardship and using what one has in hand is the readings' understanding of the co-creative nature of the soul. Ultimately, each of us is challenged to work in conjunction with the divine force and our universal calling to bring spirit into the earth, not necessarily wealth.

Material gains cannot be an end unto themselves. Nor can the desire for material gain alone propel the necessary economic healing. Instead, the readings' premise is that any economic challenge faced by an individual is inextricably connected to a personal lesson or an opportunity to apply spiritual or universal laws in everyday life. Rather than seeing financial hardships as some sort of punishment or mistakenly assuming that the experience of poverty can somehow make someone more "spiritual," the Cayce readings suggest that, when seen correctly, the process of achieving economic healing can embody a worthwhile experience in personal growth and improving our relationships at all levels. Approaching these lessons, both in gratitude and with the proper intent, can speed up the learning process.

Contemporary society, including much of the "New Thought" movement, often presents the intention for achieving economic healing and overcoming financial challenges as the attainment of personal abundance and prosperity. With this approach, getting money is sometimes viewed as a "trick" we can play with the cosmic forces, as we learn how to manipulate our "vibrations" in an attempt to activate the "law of attraction." This is not the perspective found in the Cayce readings. What is perhaps the greatest lesson in the Cayce material on economic health is that he approaches it through the ideal of relationships rather than through the spiritual mechanics of personal manifestation.

The readings suggest that a true understanding of abundance and prosperity is the mindset that although there is no lack in spirit, everything is ultimately a part of the Creative Force. Each individual is entitled to that which is necessary to his or her personal development. Oftentimes, the readings encouraged people to "be content" with what they had "but never satisfied." In other words, they were to have an understanding that there was a purposefulness to their present situation but, at the same time, they could grow and learn from that situation by working with spiritual principles, self, and the importance of assisting others. It is also important to suggest that real abundance is not so much what we possess in terms of personal resources, but what we embody and put out into the world through our understanding of manifesting spiritual principles.

By working with the readings' principles on economic healing, many individuals and groups have found the Edgar Cayce information extremely helpful. The approach for achieving personal material success is about much more than money. It is an approach that encourages individuals to use what they have in hand and to discover and live out their life's mission. It is an approach that admonishes people to become good stewards of the resources they have been entrusted with, and ultimately to be able to use every experience encountered in life to become all that they were meant to be.

23

The Akashic Records

A TERM FREQUENTLY DISCUSSED BY THE EDGAR CAYCE READINGS THAT had a tremendous impact upon his work was the phrase "the Akashic Records." Derived from the Sanskrit word "Akasha," which means boundless space, the Akashic Records might best be understood as the universe's Internet "Cloud" or a supercomputer memory system that keeps track of everything. Edgar Cayce suggested that the story of our lives—our thoughts, our words, our deeds, and our relationships—are stored in these Akashic Records, which served as the ultimate source of information for his psychic readings. However, these records are much more than simply a compilation of the past; instead, they are interactive and somehow draw together experiences and relationships specifically needed by each individual for her or his personal growth and development. Obviously, free will enables individuals to decide whether or not they are willing to learn whatever lesson has been presented, but the lesson is theirs nonetheless. Ultimately, the Akashic Records are each soul's "safety net," insuring that everyone will eventually have the opportunity to become all that he or she was meant to be.

Also called "the Book of Life," "God's Book of Remembrance," or even an aspect of Divine mind, on numerous occasions during the process of giving a reading, Edgar Cayce became aware of what happened to his own consciousness as he tuned into these records:

> "I see myself as a tiny dot out of my physical body, which lies inert before me. I find myself oppressed by darkness and there is a feeling of terrific loneliness. Suddenly, I am conscious of a white beam of light. As this tiny dot, I move upward following the light, knowing that I must follow it or be lost.
>
> "As I move along this path of light I gradually become conscious of various levels upon which there is movement. Upon the first levels there are vague, horrible shapes, grotesque forms such as one sees in nightmares. Passing on, there begin to appear on either side, misshapen forms of human beings with some part of the body magnified. Again there is change and I become conscious of gray-hooded forms moving downward. Gradually, these become lighter in color. Then the direction changes and these forms move upward and the color of the robes grows rapidly lighter. Next, there begin to appear on either side vague outlines of houses, walls, trees, etc., but everything is motionless.
>
> "As I pass on, there is more light and movement in what appear to be normal cities and towns. With the growth of movement I become conscious of sounds, at first indistinct rumblings, then music, laughter, and singing of birds. There is more and more light, the colors become very beautiful, and there is the sound of wonderful music. The houses are left behind, ahead there is only a blending of sound and color. Quite suddenly I come upon a hall of records. It is a hall without walls, without ceiling, but I am conscious of seeing an old man who hands me a large book, a record of the individual for whom I seek information."
>
> *(294-19, Report File)*

Rather than being a literal "place," the readings suggested that this experience was essentially a symbolic representation of his accessing information at higher levels of consciousness. Once given the record, Cayce had the ability to select the information that would be most capable of assisting the individual at that moment in life. Frequently, the readings pointed out that not everything available was being provided but instead only that information which would be "most helpful and hopeful." If another reading was obtained later, inevitably the Cayce source would provide additional insights helpful to the individual.

For ease of understanding, the Akashic Records might be conceived as containing three very different components: those records dealing with the *past* (including past lives), those records influencing *present* experiences and relationships, and those records analyzing the ever-evolving *future*.

In terms of the past, the information stored within the Akashic Records is essentially related to memory. One example of how accessing this memory can be experienced has been discussed in the phenomenon known as the near-death experience (NDE). Ever since Raymond Moody's bestseller, *Life After Life*, originally published in 1975, countless examples of NDE's have appeared online, in print, and in the media. One of the commonalities among many of these stories is that individuals encounter a "life review"—seeing glimpses of their entire lifetime flash before them. Ultimately, what is occurring in this process is that these people are experiencing their own Akashic Records of the past. These records also include memory from previous lifetimes as well as the overall accumulation of a soul's talents, experiences, inclinations, and desires.

Edgar Cayce's secretary, Gladys Davis, told members of the office staff that she had an intense phobia of sharp, cutting instruments such as knives and scissors. She stated that throughout her life she had often been gripped by "nervous fear" whenever she saw a sharp instrument near her or witnessed someone else using one. She eventually came to understand this fear as part of a past-life memory: according to Edgar Cayce's own readings for her, in ancient Persia she had been killed by being run through with a sword. Once she understood where the fear came from, it began to diminish, and she no longer had an issue with it.

As discussed in Chapter 9, a unique concept from the Cayce information is that past-life "karma" is essentially memory—it is memory from the past that the individual encounters (and deals with) in her or his present-life experiences and relationships. We all have examples of this kind of memory—we have certain occupations we are drawn to, or specific kinds of foods we like, or cultures and historical timeframes that appeal to us. Those things that seem to be an innate part of who we are can oftentimes be traced to karmic memory. Other examples include meeting someone for the very first time and not liking that person, or meeting someone and having an instant positive attraction to that individual. Edgar Cayce stated that we pick up all of our relationships, our talents, our animosities, and our shortcomings exactly where we left them off.

In regards to the Akashic Records of the present, the readings suggest that each of us has an almost unlimited number of patterns from the past (both positive and negative) that can be "re-energized" by our thoughts, activities, and relationships in the present. Some of these patterns relate to positive qualities and talents, while others deal with negative behaviors and shortcomings. Each of these is essentially the byproduct of what the soul has done with its prior experiences. For example, an innate musical talent is simply the individual picking up an ability that was acquired previously. Conversely, an innate negative behavior, such as selfishness, aggression, bigotry, etc., can be a shadow of negative choices and experiences from the past. What's important for us to become aware of in the present is that it is just as easy to energize a negative pattern by our thoughts and activities as it is a positive one. That is why the Cayce information frequently recommended working with spiritual ideals.

From Cayce's perspective, each of us clearly sees our own strengths and weaknesses in other people. And we often deal with our karmic memory (both positive and negative) in our relationships with others. Ultimately, the Akashic Records draw to us people that mirror our own strengths and weaknesses, following the universal law: "Like attracts like." Each of us sees in other people something very specific to our own needs.

The Edgar Cayce readings clearly state that each relationship and every experience that we find ourselves involved with in the present has the potential to be helpful and hopeful in terms of the soul's quest for personal wholeness. Cayce saw the earth as a "cause and effect" classroom whereby each individual constantly has the opportunity to meet self and apply spiritual principles in the material world. Differing than some New Age schools of thought, rather than "getting out of the earth," the readings' premise is that our ultimate goal is to bring spirit *into* the earth, manifesting the individuality of the soul in the process. Our success with those lessons and relationships determines the next series of experiences that our soul draws to us. Actually, each choice in the present leads to another series of potential futures.

For example, if a soul really messes up in the present—totally ignoring the lessons that are being presented and becoming abusive (or even criminal) in relationship to others—the next time around, that soul will have much more limited parameters of free will. Ultimately, the universe will only let a soul get into so much trouble. Conversely, a soul that really achieves lessons on its learning agenda will be given much greater flexibility and much greater parameters of free will in which to bring "spirit into the earth." Our personal free will is inextricably connected to how well we interact with the lessons that the Akashic Records draws to us.

The Akashic Records of the future embody an ever-changing array of possibilities and potentials. The future is not fixed; instead, the future changes and alters with every thought, every choice, and every decision we make in the present. Essentially, the future is an ever-evolving shadow of that which may be, totally dependent upon what one does in the present with what he or she has learned from the past. However, because we are constantly receiving information from the Akashic Records, essentially "tapping into" the material connected to us personally, our changing futures can be glimpsed in intuitive impressions, hunches, and even our dreams. In fact, the Cayce readings state that nothing of significance ever happens to anyone without it first being foreshadowed in a dream.

Because of the nature of the Akashic Records and the fact that they are responsible for drawing to every soul exactly what that soul needs, the Akashic Records are constantly calculating probabilities—if the individual does this, this is the probable outcome; if someone makes this choice, this is where it is potentially headed. As we sleep, we often tune into the superconscious mind and our own potential futures. This is exactly what Cayce meant by seeing a shadow of the future in the dream state.

For example, many individuals have had the experience of having a conversation with someone, or going somewhere, and all at once having the realization, "What a minute—I've already had this conversation . . . " Or, "I've already been here . . . " These experiences of déjà vu happen most often because an individual dreamed about the activity previously, and while it is occurring there is a partial memory of having encountered it before. This kind of déjà vu is essentially associated with tuning into higher levels of consciousness.

Aaron Frazier was a thirty-year-old businessman when he had a dream that seemed to indicate a change in his company's table of organization. His boss had left the company, making him one of the applicants in line for the job opening, which would have meant a promotion. While waiting for the decision to be made, he had this dream.

"I saw the table of organization on the company president's desk. As if somehow watching over his shoulder, I saw the president use a pencil eraser to erase the entire division that had once reported to my boss, and separate it into two different departments. Using his pencil, he then connected one of the departments to an already existing division within the company, and then he connected the other department to another division."

Within a week, the company announced that the departing division director would not be replaced. Instead, as a cost-savings measure, the company had decided to break apart the division and separate its functions between existing divisions within the corporation. As a result, the dreamer retained his job, but ended up reporting to another division director, just as had been foreshadowed in his dream.

The Akashic Records are much more than a memory storehouse of data, these records are interactive in that they have a tremendous influence upon us in the present as well as upon our unfolding futures. We constantly interact with them, and they download those very circumstances and experiences we need to become better people. The records are our personal tool for keeping track of the lessons we've learned and still need to master on the soul's wholeness curriculum. In fact, Edgar Cayce stated that each of us is where we are for a reason: it has been pulled together by the Akashic Records themselves.

A good example of the activity of the records comes from the story of Kelly, who had a dream of them as a "tablet." Kelly was participating in a dream incubation project at a summer camp program by spending a day in isolation and then a night in a special "dream tent" erected for this purpose on the banks of the nearby creek. She had been praying for information concerning the direction of her career. The next morning, she had this report:

> I awoke in the middle of the night, startled to find that a strong wind was blowing, and that the dream tent had blown away! A small, old woman appeared, calling out my name, and commanded me to pay attention to what was about to happen. She said she was preparing my body for death and that the winds were spirits which would pass through me to check the seven glands. I was at first afraid, then took comfort in the old woman's aura of confidence and authority. Finally I surrendered to the experience. At that time, I saw before me a large luminous tablet, containing many columns of fine print which detailed my past experiences and my future lives. This vision ended abruptly, and I found myself lying within the tent as if I had awakened from a dream. This experience was very different, however, from any other dreams. Over time, I had other dreams that commented on this vision, and gave me the confidence to choose a new, more creative path for my career.

From what source do such dreams draw their information, not to mention the creative intelligence to gather the "just so" information to apply toward an ingenious purpose? In today's language of quantum physics, Ervin Laszlo has compiled and shared the scientific version of Cayce's Akashic vision in his well-regarded book *Science and the Akashic Field: An Integral Theory of Everything*. He explains that just as there are invisible but highly active electro-magnetic fields and gravitational fields, there exists also an informational field. One of the primary observations in modern science that require the acceptance of this ancient Hindu notion is that of "non-locality." This term refers to what Einstein called "action at a distance," or the instant transmission of information over large distances, as when a pair of widely separated electrons maintain an instant rapport connecting the polarity of their spin. More than this "psychic" connectivity, Laszlo goes on to explain how this informational field acts with intelligence and purpose, providing a guidance system for the evolution of creation, especially that of consciousness itself. The direction of the evolution of consciousness, according to the evidence, is away from an ego-centric point of view to a more transpersonal orientation.

Whether considered from the point of view of Cayce's psychic vision or from the perspective of integral science, if the Akashic Records are the mind of God, then that God is one that actively cares that we "wake up" to the underlying reality of our existence.

Ultimately, where is all of this leading? Why are we supposed to be working on loving one another and dealing with issues we have with ourselves and one another? The answer is really so that we can become worthy companions of an all-loving Creator. The soul is destined to grow (and eventually awaken) to an awareness of its true relationship to the Creator. Whatever it takes to bring about this growth in consciousness is exactly what the Akashic Records will continually draw toward the soul. Cayce asked one individual, "Can the will of man continue to defy its Maker?" (826-8) It is just a matter of time before we all join up in a sense of shared companionship, a destiny that is already written in the book of remembrances.

24

Appreciating Your Mission in Life

ALL OF LIFE IS MEANINGFUL. ACCORDING TO THE EDGAR CAYCE PERSPECTIVE, everything that exists—all experiences, all human interaction, even all of our personal challenges, are potentially meaningful. Your personal life is also meaningful and has a purpose, a purpose that involves other people. The Cayce readings indicate that as long as we are in the earth, we have a personal mission to fulfill—even when the challenges of life might make us question our personal worth, value, or effectiveness.

During those occasions when the challenges of life seem to appear more monumental than the beauty of it, we might want to recall the fictitious character George Bailey, whose story was enacted by Jimmy Stewart in the classic movie, *It's a Wonderful Life*. Faced with seemingly insurmountable difficulties, George doubts that he can make any difference and believes that folks would be better off if he were dead. An angel comes to visit George and gives him a vision of what life in his town would have been like had he never been born. George is amazed to discover just how different, how disappointing, how unfortunate life circumstances are for many people in his hometown that never had a George Bailey living there. The vision enlightens George that his life does indeed have meaning, and that his interactions with others have made a tremendous difference in the world. To describe George's mission in life, we wouldn't so much focus on his being a banker, but instead on his compassion and empathy and the ways he interacts with and helps other people—even his attitude affects others. Although the story is fiction, George Bailey's life does serve as a potential archetype of human experience, showing us the tremendous value of each and every soul and each soul's impact upon the whole.

Does it truly make a difference that you are here? Of course. Cayce affirmed that each of us has a specific mission in life. To understand the nature of that mission, we have to take a few steps back from our current life to get a feeling for the larger story. Cayce's cosmic perspective begins with God the Creator and His purpose for creating the world. In that perspective, God created the universe, and us souls, for the purpose of co-creative companionship. The intent of our creation is that we would come to a level of consciousness in which we could bring the consciousness of spirit into matter. The meaning of life, in this perspective, is an evolutionary one, leading to humans being able to experience a connection with the Creator and to actively participate in the ongoing process of creation. It's a goal that involves our own participation, which is where our own personal sense of meaning comes into play as we interact with others. At one level, we all have the same larger mission in life: to become God-realized and to share that consciousness of spirit with others, through kindness and service, making the world a better place for our having lived in it. However, in addition to the grander general mission we all share, we each have a more personalized mission in life.

One's personal mission in life is a dynamic match between your particular talents and the needs of the world. It is a creative dynamic that inspires you to develop your soul qualities so that you'll have access to the gifts you have to share with the world. It is not necessarily a job description or a career path, although it might overlap sometimes with your livelihood. It is generally something that gives you such joy that you would do it even if you were not getting paid for it. Because it is an innate part of your soul being, it is something that you do very well and naturally. It is uniquely yours, even though others may have similar missions or avocations to share with the world.

Consider the case of a sixty-year-old executive housekeeper who oversaw the cleaning staff at a hospital. When she came to Edgar Cayce and inquired as to the nature of her mission in life, Cayce told her that the work she oversaw was instrumental in assisting patients in their healing process. Although she often thought of herself as a housekeeper, Cayce told her that her real mission was that of a healer—helping to create a healing atmosphere for those in need. In fact, Cayce confirmed that this being of service to others in need of healing had been a part of her soul's unique purpose for many, many lifetimes.

On another occasion, a forty-two-year-old schoolteacher was told that although her vocation was education, her real mission in life was the talent she possessed making all individuals feel better about themselves and their personal abilities. Cayce told her that her efforts in this regard would truly make the world a better place because of those individuals she had personally affected and impacted.

In terms of your personal mission in life, you are irreplaceable, for no one can serve those you contact in exactly the same way as you do. Where your unique combination of talents and personal traits match certain needs in the world, you become the only suitable response. It is your mission to plug that hole, to fulfill those needs as only you can. And as you reach out to serve these needs, your soul blossoms and takes one more step into its lively incarnation. Our personal mission in life links the needed steps for our soul development to opportunities to serve the needs of others. As in all of creation, nothing is wasted, each living element in the unfoldment of its existence shares and sheds aspects of itself—aspects that other elements in existence need for their unfoldment. One's mission in life is a way of describing this creative interdependence that gives each living being a meaning for its existence.

Echoing a memorable quote by the late President John F. Kennedy, by asking not what life can give to you, but what you can give to life, you enter into a spiritual adventure of discovery. You begin to find your "groove," where effort ceases and ease takes over, where synchronistic events multiply and give you a sense of being in the right spot at the right time. It is a process that the Cayce readings described as "line upon line, precept upon precept." Life ceases to be an uphill struggle, but is instead a thrilling ride that continually presents surprising glimpses of unknown talents and abilities.

Modern research has confirmed the existence and importance of this often mentioned phenomenon where it seems that a higher power takes over and runs things while we enjoy the ride. This research on what psychologists call the "flow experience" results from thousands upon thousands of reports by ordinary folks who participated in several long-term studies of their everyday moments. Using modern technology, researchers provided participants with beepers to wear all their waking moments. At random times, a computer would dial the participant's beeper. At the sound of the beeper, the participant made a phone call to a recorder and described for the recording what he or she was doing, thinking, and feeling at the moment the beeper sounded. Analyzing these many reports, psychologist Mihaly Csikszentmihalyi found that there was one particular type of reported moment that spoke of a special experience. The person was absorbed in the moment, at one with what they were doing, losing track of time. The activity, whether private or shared, physical, mental, or interactional, was something the person was familiar with, something of an interesting challenge, but the person felt more than equal to the task, confident, relaxed. It felt to the person as if the activity were going on all by itself, requiring no special effort on the person's part. The person felt in touch with their real self, intuitive, and they found perfect meaning in the moment. In such popular books as *Flow: The Psychology of Optimal Experience, Finding Flow: The Psychology of Engagement with Everyday Life,* and *Creativity: The Psychology of Discovery and Invention,* Csikszentmihalyi has described in detail the qualities of this frame of mind—what creates it, and what it creates—both in the life of the person experiencing it, and in the impact in the environment. Most importantly, he found that in these moments of *flow,* the person feels as if they were where they were meant to be, doing what they were meant to be doing. Flow provides for self-realization in the context of interacting with the environment. In such moments, people report losing the sense of separation of self and the outer world. Cayce's perspective on our mission in life provides an important clue on how to promote flow experiences in one's life, extending them beyond the moment.

A crucial aspect of what the Cayce readings have to share with us about the sense of mission in life is that it is not meant to be a path to private fulfillment, although following one's mission is very fulfilling personally. Instead, our having a mission in life reflects the soul's need for an outlet to serve others as a means of stimulating the growth of the soul's qualities. Just as altruism often stimulates people to reach out and extend themselves beyond their normal level of ability and functioning, so the urge to serve the needs of others is the trigger that can stimulate the evocation of dormant talents. In other words, we don't self-actualize for our own sake, even though we are often so motivated. Instead, the soul realizes that its actualization serves a larger purpose, to be of help to others and their growth toward God awareness. Rather than seeing the path to heaven as a ladder we climb solo through personal meditation and enlightenment, the Cayce perspective views the path to heaven as a large dance in which we are all helping one another prepare ourselves to be God-realized and communal citizens of heaven. We get to heaven, as Cayce often reminds us, leaning on the shoulder of someone we have helped.

Besides developing the fruits and gifts of the Spirit, which is a part of our general mission, what can we do to have a relationship with our personal mission in life? Having a relationship with the sense of mission is probably a better notion than "finding" one's mission, because relationship implies an ongoing process rather than a singular event of discovery. Our entire life's journey is our mission, suggesting more a process than an end result or product. When considering lessons from past lives, it is not so much "who" we were that matters, but our attitude, intentions, and actions that define our soul.

There was a man who was frustrated because he felt that he had failed his mission to be a famous author. Studying the Cayce material on mission in life, he realized that when he took into account, not just his abilities, but also his likes and dislikes, he realized that being a famous author was a too restrictive vision for his mission. Instead he realized that he held a fundamental idea of freedom in service. As he expressed it in his mission statement, he aimed to wake up every morning feeling as if it were the weekend, eager to get up and return to an engaging creative task, ending the day knowing he had helped someone, and enjoying his evening with family and friends. By changing his concept of mission in life from a job description to a description of a style of life, he more accurately reflected the Cayce perspective on mission in life.

And so it is with our mission in life, that it is less important "who" we become, in the sense of a career or job title, as it is the style and spirit in which we live. Discovering our mission is an ongoing learning process of discovering our own divinity. A good morning meditation that expresses this approach to spirituality might be to ask upon awakening, "What opportunity will I have today to develop my soul qualities by being of service to someone in need?"

We certainly must examine our talents and abilities to get a sense of our mission, but we must also look to our desires and what gives us joy. Surprisingly, research backs up the validity of the slogan made famous by Joseph Campbell in his attempts to educate us about the spiritual messages in mythology: "follow your bliss." In his research on flow, Csikszentmihalyi found that during those special moments, people were pursuing activities that they enjoyed doing for their own sake rather than activities that were pursued because of the anticipated results. Someone who says they'd do their work even if they were not getting paid for it is someone whose work is in line with their mission in life, for it is to be enjoyed for its own sake.

At first, we may serve others from a sense of religious duty. As we mature, however, and begin to realize our soul's talents, we exercise these talents for the pure joy of it, and we find that serving others with our talents is itself a joyful experience. It is a credit to the Creator to come up with a design that has us follow our bliss to discover the talents we have to serve others and help them grow, meanwhile discovering our oneness with God in the process. It's a good life.

References and Recommended Reading

Association for Research and Enlightenment, Inc. *A Search for God, Books I & II (50th Anniversary Edition)*. Virginia Beach, Va.: A.R.E. Press, 2007.

Baraff, Carol A. *Edgar Cayce's Everyday Health: Holistic Tips, Remedies & Solutions*. Virginia Beach, Va.: A.R.E. Press, 2011.

Bowman, Carol. *Children's Past Lives*. New York: Bantam Books, 1997.

Bro, Harmon Hartzell, PhD. *Edgar Cayce: A Seer Out of Season*. Virginia Beach, Va.: A.R.E. Press, 2011.

Bucke, Richard Maurice. *Cosmic Consciousness: A Study in the Evolution of the Human Mind*. New York: Dutton, 1959.

Cayce, Edgar. *Earth Changes: Historical, Economical, Political, and Global* (an "Edgar Cayce series" book). Virginia Beach, Va.: A.R.E. Press, 2012.

Cayce, Edgar. *Spiritual Healing for Personal Prosperity* (an "Edgar Cayce series" book). Virginia Beach, Va.: A.R.E. Press, 2011.

Cayce, Hugh Lynn. *Edgar Cayce on Overcoming Fear and Anxiety*. Virginia Beach, Va.: A.R.E. Press, 2004.

Cerminara, Gina. *Many Mansions*. New York: Signet (Penguin Group), 1999.

Christy, Lynn Sparrow. *Beyond Soul Growth: Awakening to the Call of Cosmic Evolution*. Virginia Beach, Va.: A.R.E. Press, 2013.

Cohen, Andrew. *Evolutionary Enlightenment: A New Path to Spiritual Awakening*. New York: Select Books, 2011.

Csikszentmihalyi, Mihaly. *Creativity: The Psychology of Discovery and Invention*. New York: Harper, 2013.

Csikszentmihalyi, Mihaly. *Finding Flow: The Psychology of Engagement with Everyday Life*. New York: Basic Books, 1998.

Csikszentmihalyi, Mihaly. *Flow: The Psychology of Optimal Experience*. New York: Harper, 2008.

Donnelly, Ignatius. *Atlantis: The Antediluvian World*. New York: Harper & Brothers, 1949.

Edinger, Edward. *The Creation of Consciousness: Jung's Myth for Modern Man (Studies in Jungian Psychology)*. Toronto: Inner Vision Publishing, 1984.

Ferguson, Marilyn. *The Aquarian Conspiracy*. Los Angeles, Calif.: J.P. Tarcher, Inc., 1980.

Foundation for Inner Peace. *A Course in Miracles*. Mill Valley, Calif.: Foundation for Inner Peace, 2008.

Horowitz, Mitch. *Occult America: White House Seances, Ouija Circles, Masons, and the Secret Mystic History of Our Nation*. New York: Bantam, 2009.

Horowitz, Mitch. *One Simple Idea: How Positive Thinking Reshaped Modern Life*. New York: Crown, 2014.

Jung, C.G. *Aion: Researches into the Phenomenology of the Self (Collected Works, Vol. 9, Part 2)*. New Jersey: Princeton University Press, 1979.

Jung, C. G. *Memories, Dreams, Reflections*. New York: Vintage, 1986.

Kirkpatrick, Sidney D. *Edgar Cayce: An American Prophet*. New York: Riverhead Books, 2000.

Laszlo, Ervin. *Science and the Akashic Field: An Integral Theory of Everything*. Rochester, Vt.: Inner Traditions (Bear & Company), 2007.

Laszlo, Ervin. *The Self-Actualizing Cosmos: The Akasha Revolution in Science and Human Consciousness*. Rochester, Vt.: Inner Traditions, 2014.

McGarey, William A., MD. *The Edgar Cayce Remedies*. New York: Bantam, 1983.

Mcintosh, Steve. *Integral Consciousness and the Future of Evolution*. New York: Continuum, 2007.

Mcintosh, Steve. *Evolution's Purpose: An Integral Interpretation of the Scientific Story of Our Origins*. New York: Select Books, 2012.

Moody, Raymond. *Life After Life*. New York: HarperOne (HarperCollins), 2001.

Moss, Robert. *The Secret History of Dreaming*. Novato, Calif.: New World Library, 2010.

Pruett, David. *Reason and Wonder: A Copernican Revolution in Science and Spirit*. Santa Barbara, Calif.: Praeger, 2012.

Puryear, Herbert, B. *The Edgar Cayce Primer*. New York: Bantam Books, 1982.

Reed, Henry. *Awakening Your Psychic Powers*. New York: St. Martin's Press, 1996.

Reed, Henry. *Edgar Cayce on Mysteries of the Mind*. New York: Warner Books, 1989.

Reed, Henry. *Edgar Cayce on Channeling Your Higher Self*. Virginia Beach, Va.: A.R.E. Press, 2007.

Reed, Henry, editor. *Sundance Community Dream Journal (1976-1979)*. Virginia Beach, Va.: Atlantic University, 1977–1979.

Reed, Henry. *Dream Solutions! Dream Realizations: The Original Edgar Cayce Dream Quest Guidebook*. Mouth of Wilson, Va.: Hermes Home Press, 2009. (Lulu.com/content/570130)

Reed, Henry. *Dream Medicine: Learning How to Get Help from Our Dreams*.

Mouth of Wilson, Va.: Hermes Home Press, 2010. (Lulu.com/content/568563)

Reed, Henry. *Sharing the Intuitive Heart: A Manual of Training Resources.* Mouth of Wilson, Va.: Hermes Home Press, 2012. (Lulu.com/content/12578898)

Reed, Henry, and Brenda English. *The Intuitive Heart: How to Trust Your Intuition for Guidance and Healing.* Virginia Beach, Va.: A.R.E. Press, 2000.

Rhine, Louisa E. *Hidden Channels of the Mind.* New York: William Morrow, 1961.

Seligman, Martin, E. P. *Learned Optimism: How to Change Your Mind and Your Life.* New York: Vintage, 2006.

Stevenson, Ian. *Twenty Cases Suggestive of Reincarnation.* Richmond, Va.: William Byrd Press, 1974.

Sugrue, Thomas. *There Is a River: The Story of Edgar Cayce.* Virginia Beach, Va.: A.R.E. Press, 1997.

Tart, Charles T. *The End of Materialism: How Evidence of the Paranormal Is Bringing Science and Spirit Together.* Oakland, Calif.: New Harbinger Publications, 2009.

Thurston, Mark. *Discovering Your Soul's Purpose.* Virginia Beach, Va.: A.R.E. Press, 1984.

Todeschi, Kevin J. *The Best Dream Book Ever: Accessing Your Personal Intuition and Guidance.* Virginia Beach, Va.: Yazdan Publishing, 2013.

Todeschi, Kevin J. *Edgar Cayce on the Akashic Records.* Virginia Beach, Va.: A.R.E. Press, 1998.

Todeschi, Kevin J. *Edgar Cayce on Reincarnation and Family Karma.* Virginia Beach, Va.: Yazdan Publishing, 2011.

Todeschi, Kevin J. *Edgar Cayce on Soul Mates*. Virginia Beach, Va.: A.R.E. Press, 1999.

Todeschi, Kevin J. *Edgar Cayce on Vibrations*. Virginia Beach, Va.: A.R.E. Press, 2007.

Van de Castle, Robert L. *Our Dreaming Mind*. New York: Ballentine, 1994.

Walsch, Neale Donald. *Conversations with God*. New York: G. P. Putnam's Sons, 1996.

Weiss, Brian. *Only Love Is Real*. New York: Time Warner, 1996.

Wilber, Ken. *The Atman Project*. Wheaton, Ill.: Quest Books, 1996.

Wilber, Ken. *Up from Eden*. Wheaton, Ill.: Quest Books, 2007.

Wilber, Ken. *Integral Spirituality: A Startling New Role for Religion in the Modern and Postmodern World*. Boston, Mass.: Shambhala, 2007.

Woolger, Roger. *Other Lives, Other Selves*. New York: Doubleday, 1987.

Who Was Edgar Cayce?
Twentieth Century Psychic and Medical Clairvoyant

Edgar Cayce (pronounced Kay-Cee, 1877-1945) has been called the "sleeping prophet," the "father of holistic medicine," and the most-documented psychic of the 20th century. For more than 40 years of his adult life, Cayce gave psychic "readings" to thousands of seekers while in an unconscious state, diagnosing illnesses and revealing lives lived in the past and prophecies yet to come. But who, exactly, was Edgar Cayce?

Cayce was born on a farm in Hopkinsville, Kentucky, in 1877, and his psychic abilities began to appear as early as his childhood. He was able to see and talk to his late grandfather's spirit, and often played with "imaginary friends" whom he said were spirits on the other side. He also displayed an uncanny ability to memorize the pages of a book simply by sleeping on it. These gifts labeled the young Cayce as strange, but all Cayce really wanted was to help others, especially children.

Later in life, Cayce would find that he had the ability to put himself into a sleep-like state by lying down on a couch, closing his eyes, and folding his hands over his stomach. In this state of relaxation and meditation, he was able to place his mind in contact with all time and space—the universal consciousness, also known as the super-conscious mind. From there, he could respond to questions as broad as, "What are the secrets of the universe?" and "What is my purpose in life?" to as specific as, "What can I do to help my arthritis?" and "How were the pyramids of Egypt built?" His responses to these questions came to be called "readings," and their insights offer practical help and advice to individuals even today.

The majority of Edgar Cayce's readings deal with holistic health and the treatment of illness. Yet, although best known for this material, the sleeping Cayce did not seem to be limited to concerns about the physical body. In fact, in their entirety, the readings discuss an astonishing 10,000 different topics. This vast array of subject matter can be narrowed down into a smaller group of topics that, when compiled together, deal with the following five categories: (1) Health-Related Information; (2) Philosophy and Reincarnation; (3) Dreams and Dream Interpretation; (4) ESP and Psychic Phenomena; and (5) Spiritual Growth, Meditation, and Prayer.

Learn more at EdgarCayce.org.

What Is A.R.E.?

Edgar Cayce founded the non-profit Association for Research and Enlightenment (A.R.E.) in 1931, to explore spirituality, holistic health, intuition, dream interpretation, psychic development, reincarnation, and ancient mysteries—all subjects that frequently came up in the more than 14,000 documented psychic readings given by Cayce.

The Mission of the A.R.E. is to help people transform their lives for the better, through research, education, and application of core concepts found in the Edgar Cayce readings and kindred materials that seek to manifest the love of God and all people and promote the purposefulness of life, the oneness of God, the spiritual nature of humankind, and the connection of body, mind, and spirit.

With an international headquarters in Virginia Beach, Va., regional representatives throughout the U.S., Edgar Cayce Centers in more than thirty countries, and individual members in more than seventy countries, the A.R.E. community is a global network of individuals. A.R.E. conferences, international tours, camps for children and adults, regional activities, and study groups allow like-minded people to gather for educational and fellowship opportunities worldwide.

A.R.E. conferences, international tours, camps for children and adults, regional activities, and study groups allow like-minded people to gather for educational and fellowship opportunities worldwide.

A.R.E. offers membership benefits and services that include a quarterly body-mind-spirit member magazine, Venture Inward, a member newsletter covering the major topics of the readings, and access to the entire set of readings in an exclusive online database.

Learn more at EdgarCayce.org.

EDGARCAYCE.ORG